# The Self-Employment Survival Guide

*Proven Strategies to Succeed as Your Own Boss*

Jeanne Yocum

*Foreword by Rieva Lesonsky, Small Business Expert
and Founder of SmallBizDaily.com*

ROWMAN & LITTLEFIELD
Lanham • Boulder • New York • London

Published by Rowman & Littlefield
A wholly owned subsidiary of The Rowman & Littlefield Publishing Group, Inc.
4501 Forbes Boulevard, Suite 200, Lanham, Maryland 20706
www.rowman.com

Unit A, Whitacre Mews, 26-34 Stannary Street, London SE11 4AB

Distributed by NATIONAL BOOK NETWORK

British Library Cataloguing in Publication Information Available

**Library of Congress Cataloging-in-Publication Data**

Names: Yocum, Jeanne, author.
Title: The self-employment survival guide : proven strategies to succeed as
  your own boss / Jeanne Yocum.
Description: Lanham : Rowman & Littlefield, [2018] | Includes bibliographical
  references and index.
Identifiers: LCCN 2017037263 (print) | LCCN 2017050924 (ebook) | ISBN
  9781538108727 (Electronic) | ISBN 9781538108710 (pbk. : alk. paper)
Subjects: LCSH: Self-employed. | Strategic planning.
Classification: LCC HD8036 (ebook) | LCC HD8036 .Y63 2018 (print) | DDC
  658/.041—dc23
LC record available at https://lccn.loc.gov/2017037263

♾️™ The paper used in this publication meets the minimum requirements of American National Standard for Information Sciences—Permanence of Paper for Printed Library Materials, ANSI/NISO Z39.48-1992.

Printed in the United States of America

*Dedicated with love to the memory of my father, J. Arthur Yocum.
From my earliest years I watched him conquer
the perils and enjoy the benefits of being his own boss.*

# Contents

# Mission

The mission of this book is to give people who
are considering self-employment a full view of
what being your own boss entails. By learning
about the ups and downs that come
with being in charge of your own livelihood,
I hope you are well prepared to make the best
choice for you.

# Foreword

## You Are Not Alone

For many of you, entering the self-employment zone for the first time can feel like both the exhilarating culmination of a dream come true and the realization of your scariest nightmare. Whether you have owned a business before, come to self-employment with years of work experience, or are just starting out in the workforce—you are in for a roller coaster ride. The world of business ownership is filled with surprises—both good and bad—and the key to survival is how well you negotiate those ups, downs, and hairpin curves.

None of this is meant to scare you off—I just want you to be prepared. I started my own business—GrowBiz Media and SmallBizDaily.com (with two partners)—a little more than nine years ago, after working for more than two decades at *Entrepreneur* magazine and growing up in a small business family (my father, both grandfathers, and my uncles were all either self-employed or owners of small businesses).

And as much as I learned living and covering the world of small business and entrepreneurship for all those years, I still made mistakes, trusted the wrong people, and followed bad advice. But there were upsides, too—strangers who became clients who became friends.

It may help to think of self-employment as a journey. And as with any excursion, you need a goal, a plan, and a guidebook before you head out. First, no one can determine your goal but you. Some come to self-employment because they're between jobs and need to pay the rent. Others have worked for years for someone else and reached what used to be referred to as "retirement age," but they have too many years left to "retire" or they need to supplement their income. Still others choose self-employment because they want the flexibility to choose when and where to work. Or they hate their jobs. Some are doing something they're passionate about, and they want to share (and monetize) that passion. Then there are those who plan to make self-employment the first step of a longer, entrepreneurial journey, starting small and growing large.

Whatever your motivation, the choices you make, the paths in the road you choose will be driven by your goals, so make sure you are clear about where you want your self-employment journey to lead.

Once you know what you want, you need to figure out how you're going to get there. In other words, you need a plan. I'm a big proponent of creating business plans, despite many today who'll tell you they're not necessary. Even if no one but you will ever see your business plan, the very act of creating one will help you think about what you're doing, where you're heading, and how you're going to get there.

If you've never run a business before, writing a business plan will prompt you to think about things you might not have thought of otherwise. It will force you to think about pricing, marketing, sales, and competitors and come up with a game plan of how you will tackle those areas. If the idea of writing a business plan—even if just for yourself—still seems overwhelming, look into the lean business plan concept. Tim Berry and Sabrina Parsons have written a lot about the subject—so check out their insights at BPlans.com.

Now is a good time to explore self-employment. There are plenty of places to get help—go to your local SCORE office or nearest Small Business Development Center for free advice. In addition, there are a lot of marketplaces that didn't exist two decades ago that make it a lot easier to find work, get paid, and even, in some cases, get benefits.

These marketplaces are also a great resource for you to find any help you might need. All small business owners must wear many hats. But the self-employed are particularly burdened by having numerous responsibilities while running their companies—as small as they might be. You cannot possibly know everything you need to know, or do everything that needs to get done, so consider outsourcing certain tasks to those with more expertise.

Even though my company has three employees, we are a virtual business. That means I work alone. While many of you may welcome that solitude, for me the isolation was one of the things that caught me by surprise. There are ways to get around that—schedule meetings, meet old colleagues, join a business organization, and the like (I talk to myself a lot). Jeanne Yocum addresses this concern in part IV.

Which leads to the last must-have as you set forth on this journey—a guidebook. You are, more than likely, entering uncharted territory—at least for you. You wouldn't set out on a journey without a map (in the old days) or GPS to help guide your path.

That's what Yocum set out to provide in *The Self-Employment Survival Guide*. Think of her as your Sherpa—the person who's there to make your journey easier. This book tells you what to expect, identifies the potential pitfalls, and helps keep you on the right path. As I said above, while nothing can completely prepare you for self-employment, this book makes you aware of the possibilities of what may happen and how you can plan ahead to avoid the bad and embrace the good.

Whether you're starting on this journey to self-employment driven by passion or profit doesn't matter. What's important is that even though you're self-employed, you are not alone. Yocum is in your corner—and this book will help you safely navigate your journey.

—Rieva Lesonsky, Small Business Expert and
Founder of SmallBizDaily.com

# Introduction

## An End and a Beginning

Each year when Labor Day rolls around, I celebrate with extra fervor because it was on Labor Day weekend in 1989 that I made the best decision of my career. I decided to stop being a wage slave and become my own boss. The Tuesday after Labor Day, I went to work and told the owner of the Boston public relations firm where I worked to—in the immortal words of the David Allan Coe song that Johnny Paycheck made famous—"Take This Job and Shove It."

Okay, I didn't use those exact words. It was important to leave on good terms because I was hoping the agency would be my first client as I sailed back into the freelance world that I had left nearly three years earlier. You see, I had been freelancing for about eighteen months when, toward the end of 1986, the agency owner, who had been my biggest and steadiest client, had made me yet another job offer. This, her third offer over about six months' time, was prefaced by ominous words: "If you don't take this offer, we *will* hire someone else and won't need you as a freelancer any more." In other words, my biggest client—the one from whom I made enough each month to pay my mortgage—would be gone. The salary had kept getting progressively better over the three offers, and she had finally reached a number that was too good to turn down. So I took the job.

Over the next three years, I slowly but surely began to regret that decision. If I hadn't crumbled and taken the job, I would have avoided a position where I got little satisfaction from the work, which primarily involved publicizing real estate developers and their projects. A few of these clients

1

were great, even visionary people who sought to build something of lasting value that would make a community better. But during the real estate boom that swept through greater Boston in the late 1980s, many more of our clients were quick-buck artists with egos the size of the luxury condos they were building across the landscape.

One of the clients who fell into the latter group once told me that, and I quote verbatim, "A monkey could write a press release." With a straight face, he also told us that he thought we should be getting him on the cover of *Time* magazine. I wanted to think he was joking with comments like these, but it was clear that he wasn't. It came as no big surprise that he was among the first of the developers we worked with to go bankrupt when the housing market crashed.

Even more problematic during my tenure at the agency was that the owner and I strongly disagreed on how the people on the team I managed were to be treated. The last straw was the annual review I had sat in on the Friday before Labor Day 1989, in which a talented employee who was one of our very best writers was excoriated in a way that was completely unwarranted.

As I drove home down the Southeast Expressway that evening, my chief thought was that I simply couldn't do this anymore. I couldn't continue working for clients I didn't respect and who didn't respect the people in our firm. I also couldn't continue to play the role of buffer between a constantly hypercritical boss and good, hard-working employees who were deeply un-happy about how they were being treated.

## Alarm Bells Sounding, But No One Listens

Number three on my list of reasons to leave was that it was clear by my sec-ond year of employment at the firm that the real estate market in Boston was about to come crashing down. Along with others on the management team, I spent a lot of time talking with the owner about the fact that we needed to diversify the client base. The message fell on deaf ears. The owner had always worked with real estate clients since founding the agency in 1980 and had made a ton of money doing so; she just couldn't see that this gravy train was about to go off the tracks.

I feared for my job and everyone else's job if we didn't make some changes soon. It was no surprise to me that within a year after I left, the agency had downsized considerably and was hanging on by a thread. Fortunately, the owner eventually was able to turn things around by diversifying the client base, but she had to do it with a gun to her head, which is never a comfort-able situation. In leaving, I felt like I was the first rat leaving a sinking ship.

However, by getting out early, I was able to reestablish my relationships with all my former clients before the recession hit; this enabled me to make it through to the other side of the downturn, although it was sometimes a struggle. Being a one-person agency during the recession turned out to be a significant selling point, as companies were seeking lower-priced alternatives for handling their public relations needs.

Twenty-nine years later, through the good and the lean times, I have never once regretted my choice, especially after seeing friend after friend get kicked to the curb by the corporations to which they'd devoted decades of their careers. The worst example happened to my friends at Polaroid, all of whom had worked there for most, if not all, of their careers. When the company went bankrupt in 2001, the federal Pension Benefit Guaranty Corporation agreed to make good on most of their basic pensions, but the rest of their benefits—notably the $300 million in stock Polaroid employees had purchased through the Employee Stock Ownership Plan, along with retirement health care and severance packages—were canceled. It was heartbreaking to watch.

I have also seen other friends lose jobs repeatedly in successive recessions and who, now in the latter stages of their careers, face the challenge of finding work in an era where companies value youth over experience. As I witness all this, I am very happy that I decided back then not to leave control of my fate in anyone else's hands.

## Eyes Wide Open

According to the U.S. Bureau of Labor Statistics, in 2015, fifteen million Americans were self-employed; this represents 10.1 percent of the population. Not included in this number are tens of thousands of people who, in addition to holding down a full-time job, work on their own on nights or weekends, many with the hope of eventually building a business they can pursue full time.

You too might be tempted to try being your own boss. No doubt you have your own set of reasons why you'd like to leave your nine-to-five gig and try to make a living on your own. Maybe you actually enjoy your current job but still have a burning desire to create a business of your own. Whatever your motivation, self-employment is definitely worth considering, and I hope it proves feasible for you.

Yet while I never discourage people from following their dreams of becoming their own boss, you really do need to consider all the ramifications of such a big decision. Self-employment is definitely not for everyone, and it particularly is not for people who can't stand the inevitable stresses that are part and parcel of being self-employed.

I think I was lucky to be aware very early in life that owning your own business and being the boss is not necessarily a cakewalk. My father owned a small lumber mill in Pennsylvania. Most of the time he had three to five employees working for him. The lumber business, of course, is one of the most cyclical businesses on the planet, so I saw my father struggle to stay afloat during numerous recessions. Add in Pennsylvania winters when it was impossible to get into the woods to cut timber, and you have a business that was full of rough spots. As I grew into my teens, the burden on my father of having to meet the payroll and the pain he felt at those times when he had to lay off his men was readily apparent to me.

## There's No Going Back

With this at-home example in mind, I wasn't expecting self-employment to be a problem-free existence. But over the years I've seen numerous people leap into self-employment thinking everything would be ideal if they could just be their own boss. Many have succeeded, but some have not.

I always think it must be a very bitter pill to swallow to have to go back into the employment market after failing at self-employment. A big part of me thinks that you really can't go back once you've tasted freedom. I say this after having tried freelancing for nearly two years and then having accepted what was to become my last "job." You've already read about that debacle. So what I really think is that if you're going to become self-employed, you had better make darn sure you get it right so that you don't have to go crawling back into the job market with your tail tucked between your legs.

As you consider the upsides of self-employment, of which there are many, I also encourage you to have a realistic view of the potential challenges you may face. Being your own boss is great. But there are times when it is clear that it is not the right fit for everyone. So before you dash into your boss's office and sing your own rendition of "Take This Job and Shove It," read about the challenges of self-employment that I've experienced or witnessed friends and colleagues experience. And take heed of how we overcame these hurdles with proven coping strategies.

To provide you with a wide range of perspectives, I have included comments and advice from several colleagues and clients who all have had long experiences with self-employment. Most of them work as solopreneurs, but one, as you will see, started out working alone and now has employees and subcontractors. Their varied experiences and insights should help broaden your awareness of the issues you should be prepared to deal with if you choose to walk this path. Look for these comments in the Other Voices sections of the chapters ahead. I thank them all very much for the great additions they've made here. Be sure to check out their bios at the end of the book to learn about the great businesses they've all created for themselves.

Some of the challenges I discuss can be avoided simply by knowing about them ahead of time. Others are beyond your control, but by thinking about them in advance, you can decide whether this is a risk you're willing to take. You can also do some advance preparation that will put you in a better position to deal with some risks should they come along. Also, in reading about the challenges, you may realize that now is just not the right time to try self-employment, but that there is advance planning you can put in place that will better prepare you for joining the ranks of the self-employed sometime down the road.

Now as my career winds down, I am focused on working with just a couple of clients and devoting significant time to my blog, SucceedinginSmallBusiness.com, where my cobloggers and I share advice on how to make it as a solopreneur or small business owner. As I look back at the full span of my career, which included everything from teaching elementary school to working for small businesses and major national corporations, I can truthfully say that the years I have spent as my own boss have been by far the most intellectually rewarding and happiest part. As you step into the world of self-employment, I hope that you will also be able to look back decades from now and say that same thing of your time out there on your own.

# PART I

# NOW THAT YOU
# WORK FOR YOURSELF

# CHAPTER ONE

# You're the Boss Now

I wouldn't trade my nearly three decades of self-employment for anything, but some days I do wish I had a boss. In essence, I have multiple bosses, namely clients who are all pushing forward their own agendas. Sometimes it would just be nice to have one person who was in charge of telling me exactly what the priorities should be rather than having to decide for myself each day. This would be particularly helpful on those days when the number of balls I'm juggling seems overwhelming.

Before making the leap into the world of self-employment, please carefully consider whether you're really ready to not have a boss—to not have someone who is making the key decisions or confirming for you that your decision is the correct one. Self-employment is extremely stressful if you're not a decisive person. Every day is filled with choices about the direction you're taking your business, what you need to do next to move your business forward, and about the work you're doing for your clients.

I am usually quite decisive—to the point where my friends are often stunned by the quickness with which I've made major life choices—but even I sometimes have a problem picking from among the many options I'm faced with as my own boss. If someone like me occasionally feels anxious over trying to figure out what her priorities should be, I could only imagine what it would be like for someone for whom any type of decision-making is a stress-filled chore.

Sure, you can seek opinions on key decisions from mentors, colleagues, or family and friends. But when you're self-employed, in the end it all comes down to you. You are the one who will have to make the decisions that will determine if you succeed. Will you be comfortable with this?

Some people welcome the opportunity to finally show that they can make it on their own. They've felt reined in and have been dying to be the decision maker. But plenty of others leap into self-employment without considering that the proverbial buck will now stop at their desk.

If, upon reflection, your stomach gets a little queasy at the notion of having to be the "decider," then perhaps you should consider delaying your dream of self-employment until you become more comfortable with decision-making. It is quite possible that once you get more professional experience—and more life experience—under your belt, you will become more at ease with decision-making and be better prepared for life without a boss.

If you happen to be one of the unlucky people who has a bad boss, having no boss at all probably seems awfully attractive. In fact, that was one of the top five reasons I became self-employed. I chafed under the micromanagement of my last boss. So I quit and didn't look back. If you find yourself in a similar situation, before making such a move, please thoroughly consider the ramifications of having no boss at all. If you have problems with decision-making, perhaps a better move would be to find a new job with a better boss.

If you've already made the leap to self-employment and are now struggling with decision-making, try these coping strategies.

## Coping Strategies

- **Know your decision-making style.** Some of us need to thoroughly research all our options before reaching a decision. Others go more with gut instinct. Some of us fall somewhere in between, which is probably the best place to be. Understand your style and try to reach a happy medium that enables you to move forward without getting mired in endless research or making a snap decision you will soon regret.
- **Don't overthink everything.** Some choices are so big that they deserve a lot of thought, but I know people who vacillate over every step of daily life, beginning with what cereal to have for breakfast. Don't be that person. Make choices and stick with them as you move through your workday, unless you receive information that gives you good reason to shuffle the items on your to-do list.
- **Have a friendly sounding board.** While I recommend finding a good mentor who has walked in your shoes and can give you the voice of experience, I also think it's good to talk over a decision you're facing with someone who is just a really good friend. This person will likely have known you longer than your mentor and probably knows your personality better because they've seen you in all sorts of situations over many years. Someone like this can provide valuable input that is based

on experience with you rather than on their own experience with self-employment. Listening to someone like this can be very helpful since they know your tendencies with decision-making and may help you avoid a choice you might regret later.

- **Trust your intuition.** When faced with a decision, often your first thought is your best thought. By learning to trust this gut instinct, which, after all, is derived from your life experience and your knowledge of the topic involved, you should significantly shorten the amount of time you spend dithering.

## ✑ Other Voices ✑

**Barbara Rodriguez** started her interpreting and translation services business in Springfield, Massachusetts, in 2001. I met her a few years later when her business was located at the Springfield Business Incubator, for which I was writing a newsletter.

Here's what Barbara says on being the boss: I'm sure you've heard about how lonely it is at the top. That's because you have no one to consult with. The buck stops with you, and it can be frightening. Take the time to think things through. Sleep on it. At the beginning, I would make decisions quickly and then live to regret them. It took me many years to learn to sleep on decisions, and I mean that literally. Things are always clearer in the morning. You have to think about how a decision you make today will affect your business into the future. Are you taking on obligations you can't meet? Are you cutting yourself short? How is the market changing and how will those changes affect you? Can you deliver the goods and/or services on time? Again, meditation really helps me to see all angles of a situation—and again, sleep on it!

I've known **Howie Green** since 1973 when we worked in the corporate communications department of a large insurance company in Boston. Howie describes himself as a graphic designer, illustrator, and reluctant writer, but I would add that he is a very talented artist. He first was self-employed for a three-year period beginning in 1979. Then he returned to self-employment permanently in 1984.

Here are his thoughts on being the boss: In my youth, I worked for a lot of people, and I never had a boss who I thought had a clue as to what he or she was doing. I always thought I would make better decisions than they would. And I was right, so with that kind of an ego, I needed to work for myself.

CHAPTER TWO

# Make Working from Home Work

In the mid-1980s, I did a two-year stint of freelancing before reverting back to being an employee again. I worked out of my condo on Commonwealth Avenue in Boston's Back Bay. Because some buildings on the street had been converted from residential to commercial space, unless someone specifically knew the building I lived in, they would not know I was working from home.

A number of people advised me not to let people know I worked from home. Home offices were not yet common in the mid-1980s, so these well-meaning friends feared I would look less serious about my business because I hadn't rented office space. I didn't think it was necessary to conceal where I worked, so I ignored this advice. What I found was that people didn't even ask where my office was, and those times when I did reveal that I worked at home, no one ever made a negative comment.

Flash forward to the second decade of the new millennium, when working from a home office has become so common that now when I tell people I work from home, the response is likely to be "So do I" or, quite often, "Oh, I wish I could do that." To the latter group, I am always tempted to say, "Yes, it is great, but it is not without challenges and probably isn't for everybody."

## Discipline Is Required

If you're going to set your new business up in your home, be aware that this requires a fair amount of discipline. When you look around your house, you can always see a chore that needs to be done. It's very easy to find that an hour has breezed by wherein, instead of doing billable work, you've emptied the dishwasher, put clean sheets on the bed, thrown a load of laundry in the washing machine, made a grocery shopping list, and watered the plants.

I'm kind of lucky in this regard because, frankly, I'm not much of a house-keeper! I can easily ignore household chores. But I do know people with home offices who find it very challenging to stay at their desk when, for example, they notice dust on the bookshelves or they look out the window and see that the grass could stand to be mowed.

A client once wrote to me about a challenge she'd been having with her home office that is also common. Her partner had recently retired and was now hanging about the house all day. The possibilities for distractions when you have someone at home with you while you're working are endless. I know this all too well because since 2002, I have also lived with a retired person who is at home during the day. That was a problem before we moved to Durham in 2013 because in our former home my office didn't have a door that I could shut. When we moved south, one my top criteria in a new house was that I would be able to have an office with a door.

If you have children living at home, that, of course, greatly increases the chances of being interrupted. No matter how well you school them on the sanctity of your work hours, distractions are bound to occur. A good friend who is blessed with girls who have musical talents tells me of trying to do a conference call during an impromptu clarinet practice.

It isn't just the people you live with who have the idea that because you work at home and control your own hours, they can interrupt you in ways they probably would not if you had a nine-to-five job in an office. Just be-cause you encourage friends and relations to call or drop by in the evenings instead of during the day doesn't mean they will always follow these instruc-tions. There seems to be something about the mere fact that you are "at home" that makes people think it's okay to interrupt you.

Most of us like to be as kind as possible to our friends, especially if they're suffering through some crisis and need a shoulder to lean on. Saying "I'm sorry; I'm busy and can't talk now" can be tough in some circumstances. But if you don't, you're apt to find that another part of your day has flown by without any progress on your work. So you end up working into the evening or making up hours on the weekend.

## The Isolation Blues

Paradoxically, while some of the problems that arise when you work at home come from other people, you can also suffer from isolation when you have a home office. I think that is what stopped me from setting firm rules with my housemate/now husband about when it's okay for him to sit down in my office for a chat. Previous to him moving in, I had worked at home alone for thirteen years. Many days I had no client meetings or even client phone calls, so by the end of the workday, I had spent many hours without speaking to another living being except for Jasper, the cat. He moved in with me on the day I opened my business, and he wasn't much of a conversationalist—except when it came to demanding to be fed.

If you're naturally an introvert, working by yourself at home can sometimes make that tendency to want to be alone even stronger, even to the point where you might develop definite antisocial habits. The problem with this is that if you're going to build a business, you will need to get out and network, network, network. So don't get too comfortable spending all of your time alone.

When all is said and done, though, I wouldn't trade working at home for anything. If you go into it with an awareness of the challenges I've mentioned, you will probably love it too.

## Coping Strategies

- **Establish ground rules about when it is okay to interrupt you.** If you don't establish this principle from the start, it's very hard to put your foot down later. To avoid interruptions from those you live with, set your office up in a room with a door that can be closed when you're working. If that's not possible, come up with other means for closing off the room, such as folding screens or a curtain that you hang across the entryway.

  It also helps to buy a "Do Not Disturb" sign to hang on your office door. (My sign says "Do Not Disturb. Genius at Work." That last point is a rash overstatement, but the sign gets the point across when I hang it on the doorknob!) That won't eliminate all problems with the people you live with interrupting your work, but it's a good start.

- **Develop the willpower to let calls go to voice mail.** Caller ID is a wonderful gift to the self-employed, whether you're working at home or in rented office space. The challenge is that you have to overcome what I think for most people is a natural tendency to answer that ringing phone.

  Caller ID is a work-around for those friends and relatives who simply can't get it through their heads that you're doing *real* work in your home office. I always answer client calls, of course, but I pick and choose among other callers depending on how immersed I am with work or whether I am expecting someone to call about something important . . . like what time we're meeting up for afterwork cocktails. The rest can go to voice mail, and I'll call them back when my work is done.

- **Have a heart-to-heart talk with repeat offenders.** You may have friends or relatives who just can't grasp what it means when you say you're working at home. I guess the thought that goes through their heads is "Oh, she's at home," never "Oh, she's working."

  Invite a repeat offender out to breakfast or lunch and deliver a two-part message. First, talk about how much you're enjoying working at home and how important it is for you to succeed at being self-employed. Gently—or not so gently, depending on what style of communication you normally use with this individual—work in the fact that non-work-related phone calls or unannounced drop-in visits during the day are a real problem for you.

  Part two of this communication involves letting the person know that they are an important part of your life and that you will still have time for them even though you are now self-employed. Even though it's you who is shifting to self-employment, you may find that relatives or friends may worry about what this change will mean to their relationship with you. They may be worrying that you will be working night and day and won't have time for them; a little reassurance may go a long way to alleviate this fear and to help them understand that you can't always take their calls.

  With very close relatives, like your mom or a sibling, perhaps you can agree on a set time each day for a check-in phone call. Ideally, this will be before your workday gets started or when it's ended. Or perhaps you agree to call mom at lunchtime each day.

- **Find strategies to overcome the isolation if you live and work alone.** Yes, working alone can be isolating, and I'll write more on this in part IV. This is less true if you're renting office space and have regular interactions with people in the offices around you. But when you're at home and especially if you live alone, you definitely need to develop ways to cope with the intense isolation you can experience on some days. I strongly recommend going out for at least a bit of face-to-face human contact once a day. When I lived alone, I always went out at lunch to grab a takeout salad, go to the post office, or maybe stop by my bank, where, to paraphrase the *Cheers* song, "Everybody knew my name." Just having someone say, "Hi, Jeanne. How are you today?" was enough to perk me up.

- **Recognize that you have options.** If you find that working from home just isn't your thing, the good news is that today you have affordable options that weren't available just a few short years ago. You don't need to take on the expense of renting solo office space. With options such as coworking space becoming available all across the country, you can join with other independent workers to share the expense of the office space and its amenities while at the same time solving the problem of isolation. Such workspaces also often present excellent networking opportunities that may lead to new business coming your way.

---

### ✐ Other Voices ✐

**Barbara Rodriguez:** The downside to working from home is that no one actually believes you're working. People think they can interrupt you at any time because, after all, "you work from home." I try to set strict chunks of time that I devote only to work. It's tempting to throw in a load of wash, start dinner, and get involved in a million little things that need doing. What ends up happening is that you work twenty-four hours a day trying to catch up on things, until you realize it's never ending.

**Howie Green:** What has changed for me over the past fifteen years is that no one knows where the hell I am working from anymore. Or cares. I'm home; I'm in Florida; I'm in New York; I'm in Starbucks. As long as they can reach me, that's all that matters. And since most communications now take place through e-mail or texting, it's even goofier. Recently, I completed a digital illustration for a client on a bus trip from New York City to Boston and e-mailed it to them from the bus when it was done. They loved it, so I invoiced them . . . from the bus.

# CHAPTER THREE

---

# Don't Sell Yourself Short

One of the most important decisions you make when you enter the ranks of the self-employed is to set a price for the services you're rendering or the product you're selling. Many factors go into this calculation, including the prices being charged by your competitors, your skill level and amount of experience, who your clients are (corporations can pay more than nonprofits, for example), and how much competition there is in your field. This can all be very puzzling to someone who has always received a paycheck from an employer, and it's all too easy to make a mistake and sell yourself short.

Here are a couple of the sticking points I've seen people get hung up on when they initially set their rates:

- **Overestimating the number of hours you can actually bill each week.** Starting out, many people assume they'll be able to bill every single hour of their working day. For people who are coming from an environment where they were billing their hours to clients (ad, media or PR agencies, law firms, or consulting groups, for example), this is an easy mistake to make. Unless you're involved in business development for these types of employers, it is likely that the vast majority of your time is, in fact, billable work. It's easy to ignore the fact that other people in the firm are devoting many unbillable hours to bringing in new clients, marketing, hiring, and other duties that come with running a business.

  Once you're out on your own, you are the one who is responsible for all the nonbillable activities that it takes to build and maintain a business. You have to set aside time for the new business development activities, like networking and proposal writing, that will help grow your client list. Obviously, in the early days, the time required for business development activities is significant, and while these hours decrease as time goes by, they never truly go away as clients come and go.

You also have to allow time to do billing, bookkeeping, buying supplies, and other administrative tasks that keep your business flowing smoothly. You'll be surprised how much time these activities eat up. Even mundane tasks, like driving to the office supply store to buy printer ink, take time that you didn't have to lose when you were employed by someone else and just had to walk to the supply closet to get a new ink cartridge

Finally, remember that you won't have paid sick days or paid vacation as you probably did with your former employer. So when you are calculating how many hours you hope to work a year in order to earn the annual income you desire, you have to allow for these periods when you won't be earning income. Granted, your first year or two when you're building your business, you might decide against taking anything more than a three-day weekend now and then. But as you'll see in the chapter on burnout in part IV, there are many reasons why you should start scheduling time off as soon as your business has grown to the point where you're on secure financial ground.

- **Lowballing your hourly rate to get your foot in the door.** It is very tempting, *especially* when you're starting out, to set a low hourly rate on the theory that this is the way to bring in business fast. But if this hourly rate is not enough to pay your bills, you'll soon find out that this strategy was a big mistake. You'll have to work an unsustainable number of hours to make up for the low hourly rate.

Recognize that once you've set a rate with a client, it is something you're going to have to live with for a while. Yes, you can go up a bit each year or every two years, but if you really lowballed the rate to begin with—say, for example, charging 30 percent less than you should be charging to stay afloat—it will take years before you can get up to the rate you really need to survive.

Don't expect to be able to just raise your rates by leaps and bounds with existing clients; they won't like it much and may go in search of someone else who is willing to give them a bargain rate. And if the economy is in trouble, don't expect to be able to raise your rates at all because your clients will be hurting financially and won't be willing to accept rate increases. They'll be thinking that they're not making more money so why should you!

Of course, as new clients come along, you can begin to charge them a higher rate. But this then puts you in the awkward position of working for some clients at a rate that is too low while you're working with others with a better rate. It would not be unusual in this situation to become resentful toward clients who are paying less. That's not a position you want to be in for very long because it puts you at risk of thinking perhaps it's okay to cut corners for the low-paying clients . . . who are only low-paying because that's what *you* decided to charge them in the first place.

- **Not doing your homework to understand what your skills and experience are worth in the marketplace.** When you start asking people how they determined what their hourly rate should be, many appear to have picked a number out of a hat. Some people take the equally poorly conceived approach of just charging the same rate that they were billing at with their former employer.

While some people overestimate what they should be charging, it has been my observation that far more people start out undervaluing themselves. And this isn't just a problem with newly self-employed people. I've met people who have been self-employed for a while who still aren't charging the rates they could and should be charging to earn a decent living without having to work a ridiculous number of hours.

Many resources are available for researching competitive rates in your locale for your type of work based on your skill level and experience. Don't skip this step. Also, don't make the mistake of looking at average national rates and assuming that's what you should charge. Rates in many professions vary significantly by geographic area. For example, when I moved from the Greater Boston area to western Massachusetts, I found I had to lower my rate by about 20 percent. Companies in western Massachusetts were much less familiar with the services of a public relations consultant and ghostwriter and thus were not willing—at least initially—to pay the kind of rates that were typical of Boston until I had proven my worth. Within a couple of years, I was able to raise my rates a bit so that they were closer to what I had charged clients in Boston.

## The Internet's Impact

While we're talking about geographic regions, I should also mention the impact of the global economy on hourly rates for skills such as computer programming, web design, copywriting, and other work that can be done remotely. Before the Internet, if you chose to freelance, you were competing primarily with people in your region. Now, you can be up against people in foreign countries, who, for the most part, charge rates so low that it would be difficult for you to survive if you charged similar rates. (I volunteer for a nonprofit whose webmasters are in Eastern Europe. Also when I posted on Twitter that I was looking for a local web design company to redesign my blog, meaning someone in the Research Triangle area of North Carolina, I received more responses from people overseas than I did from local companies!)

Also, websites such as Upwork.com, Freelancer.com, and similar online markets, while offering you the opportunity to sell your skills worldwide, have also driven down hourly rates through their bidding processes. I quickly gave up trying to bid for work on these sites after I realized that the going rate for the type of work I do was generally less than half of what I was charging existing clients.

## Coping Strategies

- **Don't plan on billing forty hours week in and week out.** A number in the twenty-five- to thirty-hour range in terms of billable hours is more achievable and sustainable over a long period of time. Never forget that you will be doing many hours of work that aren't billable (bookkeeping, new business development, networking, and the like), so your week will be much longer than just the twenty-five to thirty billable hours.

  Trying for more billable hours per week sets you up for working long hours, which, of course, many of us do from time to time. But, ideally, this is not your normal mode of working because that will inevitably lead to burnout. And besides, many of us choose self-employment precisely because we want to have more work/life balance than many employers provide these days.

  Look at your monthly expenses, including your living expenses and what it will cost you to run your business. Don't forget to include the cost of benefits, which you will now be providing for yourself, as well as federal and state income taxes and the self-employment and Medicare taxes. Then add in a reasonable profit so you'll be able to save for retirement and to enjoy life a little and not just break even. How many hours at what rate will you have to bill a month to get to your desired monthly income?

Another approach to this calculation is to start out with the annual income that will keep you solvent and happy and then work back from there. No matter which way you do your calculating, you will still need to do a reality check to make sure the hourly rate you come up with is achievable among the clients you hope to work with. Which brings us to the next coping strategy.

- **Do your homework so that you know what people with your abilities and experience typically make in your region.** Then, you can feel confident when you tell a prospect about your rates. This confident attitude will help convince that person that the rate is reasonable and justified. If, on the other hand, you're not confident about the rate you're proposing, that insecurity will also come across and undermine your position. So don't skimp on your research or on rehearsing how to sound confident when you talk about your rates. In short, don't undersell yourself; that's not the path to success.
- **Be prepared to respond when potential clients tell you they can hire someone overseas at half your price.** Given what I've said above about the impact of the Internet, it is inevitable that someone will push back on your proposed rate by quoting a lower rate they've received from someone in India or Romania.

  Fortunately, you have a load of good arguments to make in such cases. The time difference alone adds an unnecessary level of difficulty to working with someone overseas and definitely slows things down. Also, unless the person being hired overseas is a US expat, there may be language and cultural differences that will impede a client's ability to communicate exactly what they mean or want. Yes, the overseas freelancer may speak English, but do they really understand all the American idioms that your client is apt to use or will the client constantly have to figure out new ways to explain things?

  In addition, building trust with someone an ocean away is difficult and takes time, so if your client hopes to build a long-term working relationship with the vendor they're hiring, they'd be better off doing so with someone they can meet with face-to-face.

  Also, be ready to talk about what backs up your proposed rate: your depth of experience and breadth of skills. This goes not just for when someone says they can find someone overseas to do the work at half your rate, but also when anyone questions why you're charging what you're charging.
- **Be careful how you communicate any rate increases.** Sooner or later, you're going to need to raise your rates, even if it's just to keep up with

the costs of living. Be smart about how you do this. I read an article in *Entrepreneur* magazine in which someone had written in with a question about how to do this. He planned to raise his rates beginning in January, and he was asking whether he could just include the higher rates on the January invoices without giving his clients prior notice. Well, yeah, he could do that if his greatest desire was to seriously tick off his clients . . . what a dope!

When communicating fee hikes, the best route is to be as formal as possible. I've generally implemented rate hikes at the start of a new year by sending out letters in late November. Note that I said letters, not e-mails. For me, e-mails are not for major news. And besides, they sort of invite comment, whereas letters don't (although, of course, in your letter you definitely should ask clients to call you if they have concerns about the increase).

The first time I sent out these letters, I was nervous, thinking I'd probably get a lot of pushback. I've done it a number of times now and don't recall ever having anyone react negatively. At most, some clients have acknowledged at our next meeting that they received the notice. Of course, I haven't raised my rates by leaps and bounds. Usually it's only been about $10 to $20 an hour. And, as I mentioned earlier, I haven't done this every year . . . usually only every two to three years. If you need to raise your rates significantly year after year, it means you probably didn't set a reasonable rate to begin with, which is one more reason to make sure you do the homework necessary to get your rate right from the get-go.

- **Gradually either cull low-paying clients from your client roster or get them up to a rate that is closer to what you really need to earn.** You'll find that some clients just can't afford to pay higher rates. Wish them well and bid them a fond adieu. If you happen to know someone else who is just starting out and who may be charging a lower rate than you are based on their having less experience, then by all means refer the business to them. Both parties will thank you.

If you really enjoy working with a low-paying client and believe they could afford to pay closer to what your other clients are paying, have a serious chat with them about this. You don't have to make up the difference in rates in one fell swoop, but if you can gradually move them in the right direction, it's worth a try before you write them off as clients. An honest discussion is the best way to reconcile this gap or at least make them aware of it. Who knows, they may find other ways to compensate you or make it worth your while to stick with them.

Then, of course, there are cases where you see huge potential for a low-paying client down the road. If they're working on something that may significantly increase their fortunes at some point, you may want to stick with them. Just keep in mind that you will have no guarantee that their gravy train will come in or that they'll stick with you long enough for you to benefit from their increased fortunes. I've known cases in which self-employed consultants have even taken stock options in start-ups in the hope of being part of a big cash payout. This is another option to consider if you're working with this type of organization.

Finally, recognize that some clients have value that goes beyond the income they provide. For example, if a low-paying client sends you a steady stream of good referrals that have translated into business for you, it might very well be worth keeping them around even if they are paying a lower rate than other clients. Also, if a client is in an industry where you'd like to make inroads, keeping them on your client roster might be wise, at least until you've signed up a few more clients in that industry. Or if they're giving you an assignment in an area where you need to enhance your skills, that might be another reason to stick with them for a while longer.

---

## ✐ Other Voices ✐

**Carol Savage** and I met in 1983, when we served as the public relations department at Spaulding Rehabilitation Hospital in Boston. She began her freelance career in public relations and marketing communications in 1992, and since then, we have shared numerous clients. She is my go-to person when my plate gets too full and I need help.

Here's what Carol says about this topic: If you're competing with someone in a foreign country for a piece of business, the other thing you should point out to the potential client is that speaking on the phone or via Skype with someone with a foreign accent can be very stressful. I know I have a hard time with it. It takes longer and I keep having to clarify what they are saying/what I'm hearing. Also, there are cultural nuances obviously that could be time-consuming to explain, backfill—again another potential time suck.

Also, if you get pushback on your rate from anyone, you should be prepared to give them the names of clients who are happy to speak about the relationship between your rate and the value you provide.

When it comes to finding colleagues who might be willing to work at a lower rate, you may know someone who is working part-time and welcomes smaller projects for less pay. They may want to temporarily keep their hand in the business or be trying to launch their own business and be willing to take a lower rate due to their lack of experience. It's good to share—including lower-rate business—with the appropriate people in your network . . . and they'll thank you!

**Barbara Rodriguez:** Selling yourself short is a topic near and dear to my heart. When I was starting out, a friend recommended a book called *The Secrets of Six Figure Women: Surprising Strategies to Up Your Earnings and Change Your Life* by Barbara Stanny. I actually gave a copy of this book to my project manager when I first hired her. Women, especially, find it hard to ask for what they're worth. When asked our hourly rate, we tend to shrink, not meet the clients' eyes and say something like, "Well, what do you think about $50 per hour?" This is NOT the way to do it. You have to confidently stand your ground, look your potential client right in the eyes, and say, "We charge $50 per hour." It's a kind of take it or leave it mentality. This is a rather simplistic example, but the book should be required reading for every budding female entrepreneur, or, for that matter, anyone who needs help in being confident and assertive in their dealings with customers.

**Howie Green:** With the massive technology changes over the past twenty years, a lot of what I do is no longer a mystery. Logo design . . . HA! My clients can do their own online now for $20 so why pay me $500? Nine-year-old kids now can discuss fonts like professional designers. I can't possibly compete with those trends, so when clients call me and realllllly want to work with me because I'm so swell and talented and blah blah but only have a budget of $100, I steer them on a course to do it themselves, or get their nine-year-old to do it for them. It is not going to be worth my time to sell myself short to make $100. Gene Simmons of the rock group KISS found a KISS T-shirt in a thrift shop that was priced at $3. He insisted on paying $25 for it because he said, "Never devalue your diamonds!" I think that's great advice.

**Pat Mullaly** is a talented graphic designer who has been a friend and colleague for many years. She opened her firm, Circle Graphics, in Hull, Massachusetts, in 1988 and now lives and works on Cape Cod.

Here's what Pat has to say about setting hourly rates: One of the worst things an entrepreneur can do is to "Buy the Job." It's especially tempting when you first start out or find yourself with few projects on your calendar and a sense of panic that no one will ever want to work with you again. Rather than be firm in communicating your hourly or project rate and sticking to it, you agree to work for whatever the client is willing to pay. Big mistake. Word will spread, and you'll never get the kind of work you really want at the rates you actually deserve. When a client tells you that your fee for doing X, Y and Z is more than he wants to pay, counter with an alternative. You could do X and Y but not Z. Let the client decide what gets left out of the project, but don't lower your rates to accommodate his budget.

# CHAPTER FOUR

# Managing Your Time

Every once in a while, I have one of those days when things just get away from me. For example, I recall one day when I was facing a deadline on a very important project and came to my desk in the morning with every intention of cranking out a lot of writing. Next thing I knew, it was 4:00 p.m. and between unexpected phone calls, e-mails that needed immediate attention, and a minor but time-consuming household crisis, I had managed to write one paragraph. (Okay, I confess, there was some really interesting stuff on Facebook and Twitter that day, too, that grabbed my attention. Mea culpa!)

We all have workdays like that. But when you're self-employed, every billable hour counts, so the impact of wasted time is significantly greater than if you have a steady paycheck coming from your employer at the end of the week or month. Every time I manage to fritter away a morning or an afternoon or, heaven forbid, a whole day, either my bank account feels the impact or I end up working on the weekend to make up the time.

While the phone calls and e-mails I was responding to that wasted day were client-related, it is often hard to bill this time. This is especially true when you're working on a fixed project budget. If you end up with a client who needs more handholding than you anticipated when you set the budget, you're stuck with writing off much of that time.

If you experience more than the occasional day that gets away from you, accept that you need to learn more about how to manage your time. Many good books are available on this topic or you may be able to find a course, workshop, or webinar that would help you improve your time management skills.

If you hope to stay self-employed for very long, this is definitely one challenge that you'll have to overcome as much as possible. For the self-employed, time is indeed money. Take better control of your time and you will see a direct correlation between that and your income.

## Coping Strategies

- **Take control of the little things.** It's important to be responsive to clients and to not leave them dangling without information they need from you. So if I'm at my desk, I pick up the phone when a client calls instead of letting it go to voice mail. And I answer client e-mails as promptly as I can.

  Most of the time this works fine, except when a flood of such disruptions completely takes me out of the flow of writing. At such times, I change my behaviors to reduce the possibility of interruptions. This means not opening my web browser to check on Twitter or Facebook and not responding to individual e-mails as they come in but rather answering the ones from the morning as a group at noon and then the ones that come in the afternoon at 4:00 p.m. Unless the phone rings, this gives me wide swaths of time in which to write.

- **Set expectations with clients.** When I'm under the gun with a large project for someone, I let other major clients know when they can expect me to surface again. Some people will argue that alerting one client that you're trying to finish a big project for someone else is a dangerous thing. This fear is based on the theory that you should strive to make every client feel they're your most important focus at any one time. But with rare exceptions, I find clients are very understanding, possibly because many of my clients are also self-employed and understand what it's like to juggle priorities. Of course, I do try to reassure them by giving them a clear idea of when to expect to hear from me again regarding progress on their project. And then I make sure I stick with this projection.

- **Don't fill your plate too full.** Don't take on more work than you can manage to do and do well. The stress that comes with trying to juggle too many assignments at once will invariably lead to time management problems. Instead of being intently focused on your work, you're likely to find yourself staring off into space fretting about how you'll get it all done. Sleepless nights will lead to unproductive days.

- **Make sure your office is well organized to promote efficiency.** Something as simple as having your office organized by a professional organizer so that everything can be easily and quickly found can save you time and is well worth the small investment required. This is especially true if you have a hard time adhering to the old adage about a place for everything and everything in its place. Even if you're far more like Oscar in *The Odd Couple* than you are like Felix when it comes to neatness, a professional organizer can set up systems for you that will help you keep the chaos to a minimum.

## ✍ Other Voices ✍

**Stefan Lindegaard** has been a client of mine since early 2008. He started his entrepreneurial career at about age twelve, buying and selling flowers, and then later worked with several media/Internet initiatives. His first real start-up (full time) was at age twenty-one. Based in Copenhagen, today Stefan is a global thought leader on leadership and corporate innovation management.

Here are his tips on time management: Being flexible with time is one of your greatest assets when you are self-employed. This can give you a good work/life balance, and it can help you work at the times of the day where you are most productive. It is amazing how much you can get done if you find the right "burst" versus trying to force things to get done. Know how this works for you and use it to your advantage.

**Barbara Rodriguez:** I'm very obsessive about having a well-organized office and a clean desk. I find that if I have a messy desk and unorganized files, my mind follows suit, my production suffers, and I get much more stressed out. At the end of the day, I make a list of things in order of importance that I plan to work on the next morning. I think this has always served me well, both in college and in business.

**Howie Green:** A wise man once said that if you want to get something done, ask someone who is busy because they know how to manage their time. I have been busy since 1972. I am glad and grateful for that fact, and it has taught me how to manage my time. It's a lot like eating the vegetables on your dinner plate. No one wants to eat them, but you have to, so get the unpleasant tasks completed and you will have more time for the stuff you like to do.

**Pat Mullaly:** One of the biggest advantages to working on your own is planning how you will spend your time. Recognize the best time of day for you to do your best and most productive work and schedule that time into your plan. E-mail and social media tools are great, but they are enormous time suckers. Plan your online time carefully. Prioritize tasks the night before if you can. Money-making tasks should be done first thing, and all the other nitty gritty stuff goes last. Stick to your plan.

# CHAPTER FIVE

# Keeping Up with New Skills

Ever have a conversation with a professional colleague where it becomes clear that they aren't as up to speed as you'd expect them to be on a new development in their field? For example, I take it for granted that someone who works in public relations as I do would be knowledgeable about and engaged in social media. But now and then I have a conversation in which it's clear the alleged PR expert I'm talking with is clueless about how Twitter actually works or why Pinterest or Instagram might interest their clients who sell consumer products.

Not keeping your professional skills and knowledge current is dangerous for anyone. If you're self-employed, allowing your skills to become outdated can put you at a severe competitive disadvantage. But the problem is that it's even tougher to keep up-to-date when you're self-employed because no one is going to pay you to get the needed training.

When I worked in corporate America, my employers made sure I got training in any skills they wanted me to have. This training was either provided in-house or I was sent to conferences and seminars put on by outside organizations. And, of course, I was being paid the whole time I was receiving this training. One employer paid for everything but my textbooks when I decided to get a master's in journalism at Boston University to augment my writing skills. I was even given time off during the workday to take a couple courses that weren't offered at night. Can't get much better than that for being able to add an important credential to my résumé on someone else's dime!

In contrast, when you are self-employed, any training you get is at your own expense and on your own time. Take an hour out of your afternoon to listen to a webinar, and that is one hour in which you're not earning income or working to bring in new business. Nobody is going to pay your fees and travel expenses if you want to go to an industry conference or meeting. When new technology comes along that you need to master, that definitely can be time-consuming and, in some cases, may even involve adding a new expense to your monthly costs.

## A Poor Trade-Off

Self-employed people who don't invest time and money in keeping up-to-date are focusing on the short term and ignoring the dire long-term consequences of not staying current with developments in their field. I know it's sometimes tough to add one more thing to an already busy schedule, especially when you might not see immediate payback. But take this approach for too long and clients and prospective clients will begin to notice.

Sure, if necessary, you can always outsource portions of projects that involve skills you have not yet mastered. But this involves sharing part of your income with someone else, which isn't something you really want to do over the long haul, especially if it involves skills that are becoming integral to your profession. Regularly devoting time to professional learning makes much more sense and will help ensure that you maintain that competitive edge.

## Coping Strategies

- **Set learning goals.** Keeping our skills up-to-date is something we all know we should do, but it is also something that it's easy to procrastinate about. So set a learning goal each quarter and hold yourself accountable for doing something that increases your professional expertise and your marketability. Even if this goal is minimal, such as listening to one webinar a month, you will still be further ahead than if you didn't set such a goal and just let another year fly by without doing anything to enhance your skills.
- **Find inexpensive learning opportunities.** So much information is available for free online now that cost should really not prohibit you from staying abreast of the new developments in your field. How did

I learn about social media? By jumping right in, and by reading lots of articles and a book or two! (Beware of the multitude of online sellers who want to fleece you of hundreds of dollars to reveal the secrets of social media; it really is all there on the web for free.)

Also, check out resources in your community, such as your local community college, especially their continuing education department or their small business development center, where you will find any number of courses and workshops that can help you get up to speed on topics in your field as well as general business skill courses that will help you do a better job of running your business.

- **Choose conferences carefully.** Conferences are an expensive way to learn about emerging developments in your field, so be judicious about which conferences you choose to attend. I recommend local or regional conferences over a national conference for two reasons: 1) your travel costs will be lower, and 2) in addition to any learning you might gain, you are more likely to get the added benefit of making contacts that might pay dividends in terms of building your local network. (Ignore this advice if you, like me, are able to work with clients all across the country thanks to today's communication tools. At the last national conference I paid my own way to, I gained a new client in Utah, someone I never would have met if I only attended regional conferences.)
- **Make the most of your professional association memberships.** Professional associations are great resources for learning what's new and exciting in your profession. If yours produces a journal, read it from cover to cover. When choosing which meetings to attend, pick the ones where you're likely to learn something new that would be beneficial to your business. Also, see if your association has an interest group that might be appropriate for you. For example, when I belonged to the Boston chapter of the Public Relations Society of America, we formed a subgroup made up of freelancers. Not only did this group create a marketing platform for freelancers, but we also held monthly meetings where one of us would present on a topic of interest. This group was also good for pointing me toward good learning tools and resources. If your chapter of your professional society doesn't have something like this for self-employed individuals, consider starting one.

## ✍ Other Voices ✍

**Stefan Lindegaard:** I often share a little piece of advice with corporate innovators in the context of innovation upgrade, skills, and mind-set. Although my version is specific to innovation leaders, I think it applies broadly to everyone when it comes to keeping your skills up-to-date. So here goes: When you wake up in the morning, go to the bathroom and take a deep, hard look in the mirror, and ask yourself two questions. Be very honest when answering them. 1) Do I really have what it takes to move the innovation efforts and capabilities forward in my company? (Most people end up with a halfhearted yes, others know something is wrong, and a very few people can give a confident yes.) 2) Do I have a process to stay sharp on this? Insert your own field of expertise into these questions and ask yourself whether you are on top of what you need to be on top of to truly serve your clients.

**Barbara Rodriguez:** Outdated skills or lack of skills can make or break you. There was a time where knowing how to type and write a business letter was enough. That's all changed, and if you're top dog, it's all on you because you have to monitor the skills, or lack thereof, of your employees. The most important skill is communication, both oral and written. Everything else you can outsource with the exception of knowing how to read and analyze your financials—profit and loss, balance sheet, and collections. Ideally, you should know how to use both a Mac and PC and have knowledge of Word, Excel, Power-Point, and some kind of customer-tracking software. You should be up-to-date on social media, and your spelling should be impeccable. Finding employees who can spell has become more and more difficult. The problem is that people don't seem to understand the importance of good writing and spelling. For us it's critical. We're a translation company for God's sake!!

**Howie Green:** Oh, this is a huge issue for everyone now. Technology and the skills required to use technology are constantly changing. If you don't keep up, you're roadkill. I know many of my peers who just left the field because they didn't want to or couldn't deal with technology. On a daily basis, I use an Apple computer, a Windows computer, an iPad, an Android smart phone, and a dozen or so software applications. When I started out as a designer, all I needed was a pencil and a phone.

# CHAPTER SIX

# Trying to Be
# All Things to All People

When you're first getting your business off the ground or any time you experience a cash flow ebb, it is tempting to jump at any project, even if it's something you're not an expert in or even enjoy doing. This trying to be all things to all people might bring in your initial clients or solve short-term cash flow problems, but in the long run, it can get you in trouble.

In an ideal world, you perform work that you're highly qualified to do, and therefore, you're doing a fabulous job for everyone. Also, you love what you do, and this shows in the results.

Contrast this with what happens when you take on a project that isn't really your thing. Maybe it doesn't match your key skills or you don't have a lot of experience in it. But you've managed to sell yourself to the client anyway, chiefly because they don't know enough about what the job requires to understand why your experience isn't a good fit. Or perhaps it's something you are qualified to do but hate doing.

In the vast majority of cases like this, problems are bound to ensue. Maybe you do an okay but not great job. But as we all know, okay doesn't cut it in today's competitive environment. The client is disappointed and decides not to hire you again, even for projects for which you are eminently well qualified. Worse yet, they may bad-mouth you to others. "Oh, don't hire that guy; he did a lousy job for me." Yikes!

Or in cases where you are qualified to do the work but it is something you dread doing, the outcome can be just as bad. If your heart isn't in the work, the results usually show that.

## You Can Fool Clients, But Don't

I was thinking of this a few years ago when I began to revise the website copy for a long-time friend of mine. As I read the copy she had hired someone to write three or four years previously, I couldn't believe how bad it was. It violated basic web copy rules; it featured lengthy paragraphs and language that was not the least bit engaging. It was a snooze fest.

When I realized the scope of the problem, I asked my friend who had written the copy. She told me the person's name, and I asked, "Does she have a lot of experience writing website copy?" "No. She has a lot of experience as a writer but not with websites. You were busy at the time, so I hired her instead."

My friend had made the big mistake of thinking that writing is writing, not realizing that writing copy for a website is significantly different than writing, for example, a marketing brochure. This is a common misunderstanding, so I wasn't as disappointed by my friend's lack of understanding as I was with that writer who agreed to do her website. That person was trying to be all things to all people and, in doing so, left my friend with a website that did nothing for her business over a long period of time.

## Coping Strategies

- **Never mislead clients about the extent of your skills and experience.** Know what your strengths are, as well as your weaknesses. Always remember that the client's interests should remain uppermost in your mind. Sure, it may be possible to make a quick buck from someone who doesn't know the right questions to ask you to determine your qualifications, and you may even end up doing a half decent job. But then again, you may very well bite off more than you can chew if you tackle a project for which you're not really prepared. Your reputation will invariably suffer if you stray too far from your strengths. Sure, you'll solve short-term problems with your cash flow, but the cost may well be doing damage to your long-term chances of success.
- **Build your skills the right way, not at a client's expense.** If you want to get experience in a new area, first read as much as you can or take a course or two to get up to speed. Once you have a good grasp of the subject, consider partnering on a project with someone who knows that field really well. This will ensure that the client gets a good product, you'll start gaining the hands-on experience you need, and everyone will be happy.

- **Avoid projects that will make you yawn.** Of course, there are boring bits and pieces to almost any assignment, and you just have to slog through them. But if the *entire* project promises to be tedious, you have two choices. First, you can turn down the project altogether. Ideally, you can recommend someone else better suited for the work; this helps the client and also benefits the person you propose, who might very well send you a referral in return sometime down the road.

Your other choice is to partner with a junior person who you can supervise as he/she does the tedious work while you do the higher-level planning and execution. That should make everybody happy. You'll make less than if you took on the project alone, but you'll not be in danger of doing a less than optimum job because the work doesn't hold your interest.

---

### ✐ Other Voices ✐

**Stefan Lindegaard:** Focus—and a real passion—is key for you to be good at what you can offer to others.

**Howie Green:** When I started out, I took any project just to get the cash flowing. But over the years, my work has developed a style that is uniquely my own, so now clients come to me wanting my style, which is much easier and much more satisfying.

**Pat Mullaly:** I learned the hard way not to take on a project I was not yet qualified to meet. So much of what I do involves technology and new programming. I've spent too many hours learning on the job at my own expense, when the smart move was to subcontract the work to experts who could do the work well.

# CHAPTER SEVEN

# Becoming Overconfident

Possibly one of the most important and humbling lessons I've learned about self-employment is that you can never let your guard down and ignore the need to keep on marketing, marketing, marketing. No matter how well your business is rolling along, you always need to have your eye on gaining that next new client. Don't make the mistake of becoming overconfident and thinking you can afford to let the hunt for new connections and prospects slide.

Don't get me wrong; confidence is a good thing. But overconfidence can be fatal. Make sure you're not overselling yourself on the idea that all your challenges are behind you and there's nothing but blue skies ahead. Be open to hearing input from people who have a solid basis for asking you tough questions, such as people who have experience in your field and who may be more alert to market shifts than you are. Reach out to a variety of advisers and listen carefully to what they have to say. Don't dismiss someone who urges caution as just being someone who is jealous of how well you're doing.

Being passionate about your business is one thing. Being arrogant about it is another. Failing to learn the difference is something no self-employed person can afford.

When things are going well and you're feeling really good about your business, it is very tempting to ease up on networking and the other activities you use to attract new business, especially if those activities cost money. But the truth is that client defections can happen at any time, often with little notice and for reasons completely beyond your control. A client can get sold to another company that has its own set of preferred vendors. A client can face cash flow problems that mean they have to cut your line item from their budget. A client can decide to hire someone in-house to handle the services you offer. Or the entire economy can tank and take some of your clients with it. This short list doesn't even begin to cover the endless possibilities that can cause you to lose clients unexpectedly.

So let's say a big client does disappear. What are you to do? It takes time and money to gear up a marketing effort, and the worst possible situation in which to do this is when your cash flow has taken a hit through a client defection. Of course, some new-business-generating activities, such as networking, aren't going to cost a fortune. However, it's harder to psych yourself up for the old meet-and-greet routine when your business is suddenly spiraling downward than it is when things are rolling along smoothly. Many of us don't enjoy networking to begin with, let alone having to put on that happy face when we're under the stress that goes with having a business setback.

## Steady Marketing Wins the Day

Now, is it okay to scale back somewhat on the time and money you're devoting to your marketing when things are going swell? Of course it is. But don't ever completely stop those activities that keep you top of mind with business prospects. And always stay open to new opportunities that might pop up, because you never know when a bigger, better client might be right around the corner.

Because I work in marketing, I know that self-employed individuals often do stop marketing altogether for long periods. I've had numerous conversations over the years with people who call me in a panic wanting some instant public relations because they suddenly have to ratchet up their marketing after a setback. They tend to share that deer-in-the-headlights look; trust me, you do not want to be that person.

The bottom line: Never stop looking for new business. Marketing must be a routine part of your work, even in the best of times. Take this advice to heart and, with luck, perhaps bad times will never come your way.

## Coping Strategies

- **Take time to chat with new prospects who contact you.** No matter how busy I am, I try to explore the needs of new prospects, especially if someone I know has referred them to me. First, if a friend or client has taken the time to give my name to someone, I owe them the courtesy of giving some attention to the person they referred. Secondly, even if you can't help the referred person yourself because your client dance card is just too full, perhaps you can refer them to someone else. Doing this kind of favor often pays dividends down the road when the person you refer the business to does you a similar good turn. (Also, you just never know when you're really helping someone out. Once a colleague to whom I'd referred a piece of business told me months later that at the time of the referral, he had been in a really bad spot business-wise and my referral had meant the world to him. I can't tell you how good I felt knowing that I had helped someone like that. It was good karma.)

- **Have a marketing calendar.** It's always a good practice to lay out your marketing for the next quarter or even for the full year ahead of time. This exercise keeps you focused on marketing and will help hold you accountable to keeping your marketing effort rolling. Will you sometimes skip a planned activity because it just doesn't make sense to keep spending money on advertising, for example, when you've got work lined up for several months? Sure, but having an overall schedule that you check in with regularly will remind you that marketing cannot be ignored forever.

- **Track what works and what doesn't work.** There's no use spreading yourself thin by attending every single networking meeting or jumping in on every new social media tool that comes down the pike. This approach will soon lead to burnout and turn you off on marketing altogether. So make sure you're looking at the return on investment, both in terms of money and time spent. This will focus you on what's really worth the effort, especially when you're so busy with client work that you're tempted just to ditch marketing altogether for a while.

---

### ✎ Other Voices ✎

**Barbara Rodriguez:** Working from home is a big contributor to becoming complacent. You come to rely on just yourself. Over time I've learned to understand the importance of brainstorming with others. Some of my best ideas have come from brainstorming. We all see the world through a different lens. This is why diversity is so important, both ethnical diversity and age diversity. Brainstorming and consulting with others also helps to keep your company fresh and up-to-date.

I recently had to deal closely with a young woman from Spain and was impressed with how quick she was with social media and many of the new technologies that may not be a part of my generation's experience. I am clearly a digital immigrant, where she is clearly a digital native.

**Howie Green:** I find that doing what I do is a humbling experience, so becoming overly confident is never going to happen. Life is a constant audition. Milton Glaser is one of the most successful and prominent graphics designers and artists of the past one hundred years. I recently heard him say that he went into the office of a new client at the request of the company president to make a pitch for a new brand design project. The twenty-something designer who met with him had no idea who he was and knew nothing of his work. So yeah, it's a humbling existence.

# CHAPTER EIGHT

# Core Elements of Your Success

Let's end this section by looking at the three core elements that you will rely on to succeed at self-employment. These are your core talents, your core values, and your core connections. By carefully considering these components before you become self-employed, you can leverage the power of the positive points you find and fill in any deficiencies you identify before you launch your new venture. This will help you get off on the right foot and also will help keep you there as the years go by.

## Core Talents

Very few careers go exactly as planned. We get pushed this way and that by economic ups and downs, by bosses (both well-intentioned and not), by office politics, and by rapid changes in technology that suddenly make a once-valued skill obsolete. All of these forces are beyond our control. That often is what finally drives many of us to self-employment; we're seeking a little control over our own destiny.

There is one thing, however, that no bad economy, lousy boss, toxic workplace, or technology evolution can affect: your core talents. And it is these talents that will determine your success as a solopreneur. Alas, many people haven't even taken the time to analyze what their core talents are and, as a result, aren't prepared to communicate their value to would-be clients or customers.

Of course, some of us know one or more of our core talents from an early age. For example, I knew from grade school that I could write. I always excelled at essay tests and never saw anything other than an *A* in English until eleventh grade, when the boy I sat next to got more of my attention than the teacher did. (This first-ever *B* caused family tension since the English teacher who gave it to me was my mother. My father was sure she was being too hard on me lest she be accused of favoritism. Needless to say, I never told him about the cute boy!) Anyway, I am certain that it came as no shock to anyone who knew me as a kid that I ended up as a writer.

If you think back, I'm sure you'll acknowledge that at least one of your core talents was apparent very early on. What was it? And will you be using that talent when you're self-employed? Will it, like my writing, be at the very heart of your business? If not, why won't it?

Other core talents take more time to emerge. I was forty before circumstances prompted me to realize that I wasn't just good at networking, I was darn good at it! This knowledge came to me only after I had made several successive moves to new areas where I knew not a soul but had managed to integrate myself into the business community fairly quickly. What core talents have you discovered as your career has progressed? And how will you be leveraging those to move your new business forward?

Here's the thing about core talents: No matter what ups and downs you face in your work life, your core talents don't go away or become less valuable. While the world I work in shifted mightily with the advent of the Internet, my writing talent is no less valuable now than it was back when I was writing marketing brochures instead of website copy. If anything, it has become more valuable because the number of uses a client can have for this talent has increased.

Sure, some of your skills or knowledge may become outdated due to technological advances and you'll have to gain new knowledge and skills. But your core talents—those things that really and truly make you valuable to your customers or clients—don't change. Is one of your core talents problem solving? Or relationship building? Or maybe you have an innate ability to bring together disparate pieces of knowledge and ideas to create something totally new, in other words, to innovate.

Whatever your core talents are, they should be the centerpiece of your new business. If they aren't, I believe you will find yourself frustrated, just as I was frustrated when I was working in a position in which I was spending more time managing people than I was writing. In that job, I was out of balance. Days would go by when I barely turned on my computer, let alone wrote anything more exciting than a memo. "You need to write," my mind cried out to me.

I'm not suggesting that if you become self-employed, you do not have to do things that are boring. We all do. No line of work is an endless series of joyous experiences day in and day out.

But if you haven't identified your core talents and aren't focusing on them as you choose the type of business you want to have, I don't believe you actually will be successful. So gain control over your destiny; assess your core talents and make them work for you.

---

### ✏ Other Voices ✏

**Stefan Lindegaard:** Another element that I often consider in what I do is the concept of intersections. I know what I am good at and what I like to do. I try to take two or more of these and bring them together in my work or take my talents and combine them with an industry segment (i.e., open innovation within the medical devices industry).

---

## Core Values

The second essential component of your success will be your values. These are the rules you live by in conducting your business. Sadly, many people don't take time to consider what values they intend to operate their business under and, invariably, they're faced with business quandaries that require them to make a value-based choice. Every month in *Entrepreneur* magazine, an ethics columnist answers queries from readers who are not sure what to do about a given situation they're facing. Often in reading these questions, I think the people posing them have never taken time to define their values because, if they had, coming up with the right solution would be fairly easy for them.

In the course of his work with companies around the world as an open-innovation author, speaker, and adviser, my client Stefan Lindegaard has asked many businesspeople what their values are. He and I have had several interesting conversations about the fact that when he brings this topic up in workshops and seminars, most people do not have a ready answer. In other words, they haven't taken time to delineate what values drive them in their work lives . . . and, by natural extension, in their lives outside of work as well. This lack of thought about values surprised me. Since I have a firm grip on my own core values, I took it for granted others did too.

Since I started my business, I have tried to follow the values below. Check these out and see if they would work for you and add any that you feel would help you do a better job for your clients or customers. For example, I don't have any employees; if you will have employees, you should define the values by which you will treat them.

- **Be honest in every aspect of your dealings with clients.** Always tell clients (and prospective clients) what you really think, not what you think they want to hear. If you're just going to parrot back to clients what they want to hear and not what they *need* to hear, save them some money and just shut up. Also, if something is outside your area of expertise, say so and offer to find someone who can help; don't take work you aren't qualified for with the notion that you can do a quick study on the topic.
- **Always do your best.** In the writing game, it's easy to get tired and frustrated by the time you're on the fourth draft of a marketing brochure or a book chapter. But don't just start to "mail it in." Get up every day committed to doing the best you're capable of doing that day.
- **Be trustworthy.** If you say you're going to do something, do it. On those rare occasions when you are going to miss a deadline, let the client know before, not after the fact, and be honest about the reason. Also, be absolutely scrupulous in your billing practices.
- **Treat clients as you want them to treat you.** Clients are more than just a check at the end of the month; they are people who have problems and bad days just like you. So don't take it personally if they're snippy or abrupt or not as responsive as you'd like. Don't take anything personally because it almost never is about you; it's about them and the totality of their lives, most of which you know little about.
- **Be willing to listen.** If a client wants to veer a conversation off into an area totally unrelated to your work, listen. You may be one of the few unbiased people in your client's business life, and sometimes people just need to vent or sometimes they truly are looking for a second opinion. Whatever the case, be there for your clients.

These values play out in a myriad of ways during the course of a given week. For example, I had a query not long ago from someone who was looking for an editor for his fiction book. It would have been easy for me to take on the project, but I've worked only with nonfiction. While as an avid fiction reader I could probably add some value to his work, I know there are other people far more qualified for the job. So since he was in eastern Massachusetts, I pointed him in the direction of the Boston Chapter of the National Writers Union, where I'm sure he can find someone to help him. Sure, there are people out there who would take on such an assignment even if they'd never edited a fiction book before, just as I'm sure there are ghostwriters who tell people their weak book ideas are actually great, all in the interest of getting assignments and growing their income. But that's not me.

So I ask again . . . what are your core values? Having these things clear in your mind will make it much easier to get through the average business day because the right choice will become amazingly clear when you work in a values-centered way. As in the example I gave above, choosing what to do or not to do will become a breeze. And if you have employees, they also will need to know what your values are. For example, is one of your core values that the customer always comes first? If so, employees will need to know that, and they need to be empowered to take the right actions day in and day out to put that value into action.

## ✍ Other Voices ✍

**Mark G. Auerbach** is one of my cobloggers at SucceedingInSmall-Business.com. He has been self-employed since 1987, specializing in nonprofit marketing and public relations. Based in Springfield, Massachusetts, Mark also reports on the local arts scene for a newspaper and on radio.

Here is his advice on why acting with integrity and ethics is so vital: As a self-employed person, you are your product. If you behave with integrity and ethics, you'll be respected. If you tarnish your image by bad business practices, behavior, or stupidity, that's not quickly forgotten. I protect my public image. I've seen too many people make stupid moves that haunt them for the remainder of their careers.

**Howie Green:** Most of my work has come to me because of a recommendation or due to my art and design style that people like. I work in a field where my work gets seen a lot, and that is my best advertising. However, keeping clients is another matter altogether. I always make sure that clients have a good time and a good experience working with me, and no matter what I'm going through, their experience is a good one. Like the actor on stage in a comedy who just experienced a tragedy in real life, the audience doesn't need to see your pain.

## Core Connections

The third key component of your success will be your core connections. In every successful small business owner's life, there is someone who has reached out a helping hand at a critical moment. There is usually also someone who has been unfailingly supportive, always willing to listen when things are challenging and to cheer when great things happen. I call these people core connections; they are the people who truly have helped us achieve success.

Your list of core connections will evolve over the course of your self-employment, but it is a good idea to start now by identifying the people you already know who will be able to support your success. The other thing you'll want to do is figure out how you can support them in return.

I've had a handful of strong core connections over my career—people who constantly send me referrals or who are always willing to take time to provide good advice when I need it. These are people who ask me tough questions when needed and give me that reality check we sometimes all need. They point out my strengths when I'm being too humble in a proposal. They listen and advise when disaster looms. In several cases, they are people who have offered to open their checkbook to tide me over a tough spot. Although I never had to take them up on those offers, it was very comforting to know that they cared enough to make such an offer.

Do you have people who fit that description? I hope so. I could be wrong, but I think you will recognize a potential core connection fairly soon after you meet. I think it's almost like a "separated at birth" thing; you recognize someone who could be a true ally or a kindred spirit pretty quickly. At least that's how it has been for me. I hope it's the same for you. And I hope you already know who your core connections are and you're holding them close.

Self-employment is tough stuff in the best of times. And in the worst of times, like the Great Recession, you need grit, ingenuity, and a solid support system to make it through. I believe it's virtually impossible to truly go it alone; we all need someone who is looking out for our interests or with whom we can be 100 percent honest when things are off kilter.

For this reason, when you find your core connections, make sure they have plenty of reasons to feel about you the same way you feel about them—that they couldn't do it without you. Never become so busy that you don't take time to check in frequently with these people. These are relationships you simply can't afford to lose. They are the keys to your success, along with your talents and your values. The best thing about these relationships is that they inevitably end up being about so much more than just business.

# PART II

# CLIENTS AND WORKLOADS

# CHAPTER NINE

# Having Too Many
# Eggs in One Client Basket

A few years ago, I was very worried about one of my friends, who I'll call Nancy, although that is not her real name. A freelance public relations consultant like me, at that time her client roster included two small clients who gave her sporadic assignments and one very big client that consumed roughly 95 percent of her time and accounted for the same percentage of her income.

This is a very dangerous situation for a self-employed public relations consultant because, in our world, there are no guarantees. Even if you're doing a fabulous job, a client can suddenly dump you for reasons totally outside your control—and even some that are outside the client's control, like a faltering economy that tanks their business.

I am always nervous when a new marketing person arrives at one of my clients because that often means they will want to bring in a new roster of vendors with whom they had previously worked. While things don't always turn out that way, it happens often enough for it to strike fear into your heart the instant you hear a client is hiring someone new who will oversee your relationship with the company.

As an interesting aside, I've also lived through the scenario—several times, in fact—where the new person coming in proved to be a disaster and was gone in short order. In each case, I immediately thought the client had made a bad choice. Each time I had to bite my tongue and not ask the question that was on my mind—"What were you thinking when you hired this idiot????"

Instead I quietly raised red flags with the head of the organization about specific incidents that did not make sense. In this way, I wasn't seen as just being someone who resented having a new "boss" at the client firm; I was raising legitimate issues that I knew would not make the company head happy. This worked because each time this happened I had had a long-standing relationship with the company. They already knew I wasn't someone who made a lot of complaints or had a problem getting along with people.

While I can't say for sure my red flags helped push the new person out the door in these two cases, I do believe they were a contributing factor, so I would encourage this approach if you find yourself in a similar situation. Directly questioning the wisdom of a newly made hire will probably raise resistance; in contrast, alerting the boss to specific problems is generally appreciated. If these "alerts" begin to pile up, the person who made the new hire will often realize the need to reconsider.

## Change Can Happen Fast

Truth be told, the list of reasons why a client might defect is endless. Sometimes you have advance warning that things might go south, but oftentimes you don't. Which brings us back to Nancy's case. Several years into her relationship with the firm that was accounting for the vast share of her income, a much larger company suddenly acquired her client. In such a scenario, anything could have happened to her relationship with the firm. This event occurred over the course of one weekend with absolutely no hint ahead of time to Nancy—or to any of the client's dozens of employees, for that matter—that a sale was in the works. Only the owner and his wife, who also worked in the business, knew of the impending sale.

Nancy and I burned up the phone lines with conversations in which we discussed all the possible outcomes this sudden change might have for her. As it turned out, she was given a six-month contract extension by the new owner, which actually increased the number of hours she was putting in on this client. So then she had even more eggs in this one basket!

Then, at the end of the six months, Nancy was told that her services were no longer needed, which left her client roster in very sad shape and sent her scrambling to find new business. It had been a very good couple of years financially, but now the lean times were upon her. And given that at this point the country was in the midst of the Great Recession, lining up new business proved to be very hard.

Having too many eggs in one basket, of course, is not just a problem for those of us who are self-employed. Manufacturing companies, for instance, can also face big problems if they become too heavily dependent upon one or two large customers. Without a good diversity of customers, it is all too easy for a business to be totally rocked by just one or two customer defections.

Throughout my years of self-employment, I have tried to make sure I never had too many eggs in one basket. This can be hard to do, especially if one client is handing you more and more business, as in my friend's case. She certainly didn't start out working for them with the notion that they would become almost her sole client, but on the other hand, once she got really busy with them, she stopped pursuing other prospects.

Ignoring the dangers of such a situation is very risky, and before you do likewise, I encourage you to consider the possible negative consequences. I believe having a diverse client or customer base is fundamental to long-term success, whether you're out here on your own like Nancy and me or whether you're a larger business with employees who rely on you for their paychecks. So check your basket, and if too many of the eggs are from one client, see what you can do to change that situation.

## Coping Strategies

- **Get it right from the start.** Many people begin their freelance businesses already having one big client on their roster. In this common scenario, the sense of security that comes from knowing that you will be earning money from the get-go is what prompts people to finally make the leap into self-employment. This is fine, but don't linger in that seemingly comfortable spot for too long. Immediately start to make it a practice to devote significant time to activities designed to bring in new business.
- **Keep track of where your money is coming from.** I've always tried to have a handle on what percentage of my income is coming from each client. Once I was anywhere near a point where more than 40 percent came from any one client, I knew it was time to get serious about generating new clients.

  Of course, if your dance card is already full, the question becomes how do you find time to do all the new business activities required to generate new clients, let alone do the work they will bring with them? The answer is that you need to have people you can offload work to. I've always had at least one subcontractor involved in my work. In the really good years, I've had as many as three subcontractors working on different projects. An alternative is to begin to hire employees and build a company. For my tastes, this is not what I wanted to do because

I didn't want the worry that comes from having to cut a salary check to someone each week. But you can gain many of the same benefits from just hiring subcontractors who are available when your plate becomes overfull.

## ✐ Other Voices ✐

**Stefan Lindegaard:** My coping strategy here is to work in different countries and continents. Although this is a global economy, some markets are always better or worse than others, and it has often helped me to do my business development in different regions of the world. (*Author Note:* Stefan is in Denmark and has been my client since 2008, so he's my example of doing business globally—all made possible by the Internet.)

**Mark G. Auerbach:** Always keep your client base diverse. Never have more than 50 percent of your business in one client or type of business. You can replace 10–20 percent of your client base easily, but when half or more is with one client, you face disaster if that relationship goes sour for any reason. Similarly, if you're overly dedicated to one industry and that industry hits a bad patch, you could be in trouble.

**Barbara Rodriguez:** When we started out, we had too many eggs in one client basket. A good 50 percent of our income was coming from one large hospital. I realized early on that we had to try to make it a point to diversify. After a few years, I'm proud to say that if we lost that hospital—which we haven't—we would still be doing quite well and could easily replace them. This comes in time. In the meantime, you need to take very good care of that one customer and promise them the sun, moon, and the stars.

My business, interpreting and translation, consists of all subcontractors except for office staff. We have over three hundred contractors on the books. The problem is in finding quality subcontractors, and that we had to develop over time, trial, and error. As with any business, the people are the most difficult part because you can't control their business ethics, their timeliness, and their quality. You have to kiss a lot of frogs before you find your prince or princess. At the beginning, we worked with government contracts mostly for state agencies. It was a lot of work under two state contracts, but if two state contracts went under, I would go under, so I made it a priority to diversify my customer base. We started working with hospitals, clinics, lawyers, and public schools. When you build momentum and maintain a reputation for quality and affordable service, one customer tells another, and then you can play off of those firmly established credentials and references.

**Howie Green:** I had a great client who gave me hundreds of projects over a seventeen-year period. My contact was an old friend from a previous company where we worked together, so it was always an easy relationship. The work wasn't always the most creative, but it was steady and plentiful so I got to depend on it. But I got blindsided. One day, I got the new issue of their corporate magazine in the mail, and it had been designed by someone else. I called my client, and not only did he not return my call, but I have never heard from him again. So yeah, don't put your eggs all in one basket.

# CHAPTER TEN

# When Clients Are Unreasonable

No accurate depiction of the life of a self-employed person would be complete without a few examples of clients making completely unreasonable demands. Let me count the ways in which clients can be difficult:

- **Unreasonable project timelines:** Clients who expect you to turn projects around in an unreasonable time frame are more the norm than a rarity. Part of it is a lack of understanding of everything that goes into the work they're asking you to do; never having done this work themselves, they think it's simple when it usually isn't. But another major cause of this is hideously poor planning on the client's part. Their emergency suddenly becomes yours.

  Some clients routinely set false deadlines. They say they absolutely must have something done by a certain date, but when you press them on why that date matters, it turns out there is no real reason behind it.

  It's one thing to make people jump through hoops to get, for example, a website update done prior to a major event your company is sponsoring or before the launch date of a new product. It's another thing to demand that people perform miracles just because you think it would be nice to have a project finished before you go off with your kids for spring vacation. Yes, you might enjoy your vacation more if the project isn't on your mind, but pity your poor vendor who was unable to spend the previous two weekends with his/her family because your project *had* to be done without there being an actual business imperative behind the deadline!

I've learned over the years that a certain portion of clients set short deadlines because they've been disappointed by freelancers or consultants in the past who weren't able to meet any deadlines that were set for them. Clients who have had such experiences just assume no one will ever actually meet a deadline, and so their strategy is to set extra early deadlines in the hope that the project will then possibly get done by the time they actually need it to be done. I've found that if you're able to meet a few deadlines for such people, they will be surprised and begin to set more reasonable timelines as you build trust with them.

Also under this category of unreasonableness fall the people who constantly want their projects to jump to the head of the line. They can't believe you won't be able to start their work immediately; they apparently think you've just been sitting by your phone waiting for them to call.

This attitude is particularly irritating when it is a client you haven't heard from for months. It's unclear how they thought you were keeping your business afloat while they were gone. But now they're back, and they expect you to be so thrilled that you drop your more steady clients by the wayside and get to work on their project ASAP.

- **Unreasonable budgets:** Some people love driving a hard bargain when it comes to money. They pride themselves on being able to get work done cheaply and are even apt to brag about this. And if the scope of a job changes after a budget has been agreed on, they will not want to pay extra for the extra work. Such bargain hunters don't realize that by squeezing their vendors financially, they are pushing the good ones away; people with real skills and a proven track record aren't likely to put up with being nickeled and dimed to death on every single project.

Note that there is often no relationship between bargain-hunting clients and the size of their bank accounts. I have had clients who I knew were rolling in dough try to talk me down on a proposed project budget. You can argue that that kind of hard bargaining is how they got to be as rich as they are in the first place, which may well be true. But that doesn't justify, in my mind at least, trying to talk me into cutting my hourly rate or my projected project budget. (Yes, you're reading me right; such people irritate me to no end.)

- **Phone calls or texts at unreasonable hours:** Having a home office has big benefits, but the downside is that some clients expect you to be accessible to them at all hours. They figure you're only a few steps away from your desk, so why wouldn't you be ready, willing, and able to go to your computer and read the document they've just e-mailed you—even though you're in the middle of cooking dinner. This situation has only gotten worse with cell phones and texting, which allow clients to reach you anywhere, anytime.

I'm not an early riser during the week, let alone on the weekend, so one of the worst instances of violating all social norms that I experienced was having a client call at 7:00 a.m. on Saturday as she and her husband were driving down to Cape Cod. She wanted to while away the drive by chatting about the book proposal we were writing together. She didn't even bother to ask if this was a good time to talk! When I wrote on my small business blog about red flags that a prospect might not make a good client, I heard from other people who have received calls at all hours of the night. One woman recounted being called after business hours on Christmas Eve!

Everyone who is self-employed knows that it is not a nine-to-five situation. I routinely conduct early morning or evening phone calls with clients. (I once had a project that involved working with an executive in China that necessitated phone calls at midnight; fortunately, I'm a night owl, so I was more wide awake for these calls than I was for the 7:00 a.m. Saturday call from the book proposal client.) I'm also happy to talk on Saturday if needed, although Sunday is off limits. But these nonregular-hours calls are arranged ahead of time, not spur of the moment. Clients who expect you to be available for their calls 24/7 are being disrespectful of your right to have a life outside of work.

Clients can be unreasonable in many other ways, but these seem to be the three major categories that irritate consultants and other self-employed individuals. What follows are coping strategies that you should apply in the face of such irritations.

## Coping Strategies

- **Set boundaries from the start . . . and stick to them.** Know how far you're willing to bend in the areas where problems are likely to arise. These boundaries may evolve over time and may even change from client to client. For example, if it's the early days of your solo career, you may be willing to bend further on price than if you're well established in business.

  Other variables include just how crazy the schedule is a client is asking for or how much they're asking you to lower the budget. Trimming 10 percent here or there usually won't kill you, but if someone is truly bottom-feeding for the lowest possible price, then perhaps you should encourage them to look elsewhere.

One of the boundaries I always make clear to clients is that I will not be reachable when I'm on vacation. What's the point of going away for much-needed R&R if you're constantly checking your cell phone? Seriously, they all can get along without you for a week. And if they truly can't for some reason—or if your vacation is going to be a more extended one—I hope you will have lined up colleagues who can hold down the fort while you're gone.

- **Let the specific situation and client history guide your response.** If a long-term client who has always been reasonable about the timeline or the budget suddenly finds themselves in a real bind around one of these issues, you may decide to help them out just this one time. But if a client habitually operates in crisis mode or is always trying to get a bargain price, you have to decide whether this client is actually worth having. (See the next coping strategy.) And know this: Doing a client a favor that ends up with you on the losing end of the financial bargain is unlikely to pay dividends in the future. All it will show is that you can be talked down on your price, so they will continue with this approach for each future project.

  Another factor that obviously comes into consideration is just how valuable the client is to your bottom line. I am willing to bend over backward much more for a client who is a) long-term and b) provides interesting, lucrative work on a regular basis. The odd thing is, however, that I've noticed that the biggest pains in the butt are often the clients with short-term needs and whose project fees are not going to make a significant difference in my financial well-being. I've never been sure why this correlation exists, but it definitely does, and it's something for which you should be alert. For this reason if I get any red flags when we first meet to discuss a project that the potential client is going to be more trouble than he/she is worth, I just use the old trick of pricing my proposal so high that they're unlikely to accept it. (And if they do accept it, at least I'll be working at a price that will help make up for the frustration they'll undoubtedly cause.)

- **Do not hesitate to fire a client who repeatedly oversteps boundaries.** Any client who regularly commits the types of sins discussed here (or any personal boundary that is important to you, such as someone who constantly makes inappropriate sexual comments or otherwise makes you feel uncomfortable) is not worth the distress they're putting you through. The frustration and negativity they generate will drain your energy. Even worse, their unreasonable demands may cause you to neglect other clients who aren't behaving badly.

I know it can be hard to walk away from a paying client, but sometimes it truly is the wisest choice. Perhaps the worst thing that can happen when you continue to work for people who don't respect you and your skills is that you can begin to doubt your own abilities and your own right to set reasonable boundaries. Don't risk becoming a doormat for anyone—this can ruin your self-confidence and your ability to negotiate the types of deals you really deserve.

## ✏ Other Voices ✏

**Stefan Lindegaard:** Beware of what I call "corporate beggars." Nowadays, even the big companies ask for free test runs, free tickets to conferences, or free sessions. They are not always ready to pay the real price and commit with their budgets.

**Mark G. Auerbach:** I'm very clear with clients what my business hours are. (I also accommodate the clients on the West Coast and Europe and build their time zones into my work plan.) Even though the majority of my clients are on retainer, I let them know that I surcharge work assignments on evenings and weekends; I charge for travel and meeting times; and I bill for scheduled meetings that are cancelled with less than twenty-four-hours' notice. After working with a client an hour away who would set up a meeting and then text a cancellation fifteen minutes before start time, I billed round-trip mileage and travel time. They quickly got the message.

**Barbara Rodriguez:** We seem to live in a last-minute world. I'm quite obsessive about planning ahead, so it really drives me nuts when other people don't. I have resigned myself to this now being the new normal. One of the rules I live by is that if quality is going to suffer because of a last-minute request, I try to negotiate more time. If that's not possible, I refuse the job. I have seldom had to refuse a job. If you permit shoddy work to get out there and represent you in any way, it will come back to haunt you. You have to be assertive and make it clear that you will not sacrifice quality for speed of delivery.

**Howie Green:** Yeah, setting expectations is a constant and ongoing task. Clients demand everything, and you have to be the one to tell them what's possible and not possible. It is not easy, but sometimes you have to say "Maybe" or "No" when all they want to hear is "Yes." Figuring out how to do that is different with each client, depending upon the relationship. I had a rock-and-roll production company client, and our contact with them was a guy who screamed and yelled all the time about everything. He made my assistant cry several times until I explained that he deals with musicians all day long, so he has to scream or they won't listen to him. He was basically a really nice guy who had to deal with nutcases all day long. It took me a while to figure out how to say "No" to him in way that didn't make him blow a mental gasket.

**Pat Mullaly:** I realized early on that some clients would always make unreasonable demands. Usually this was because the clients were totally ignorant of what it took to make something happen. It was my job to educate them. When I broke the project down into its basic components and then assigned time and cost to each, the client's eyes were opened, probably for the first time. "I had no idea it took so long or cost so much!" was a usual refrain. Being straightforward and honest about what was involved in making a project come together is the smartest way to avoid a crisis.

# CHAPTER ELEVEN

# Fluctuating Workloads

Many times over my years in self-employment, I've felt like a frustrated Goldilocks. My workload is either too light or too heavy, rarely "just right." Such is the plight of the self-employed. You're either hyperventilating over how much work you have to get done or feeling angst about how little work you have in the hopper.

It's sometimes shocking how quickly you can swing between these two extremes. For example, when I've been toiling on a book manuscript for months and it's finally on its way to the publisher, the sudden lull that ensues can be frightening. After months of telling people I'm way too busy and battling a deadline that is rapidly approaching, now I suddenly have days of nearly empty time yawning ahead of me. Time to crank up the new business machine again!

The same is true of going from barely busy to frantically busy. With one phone call, a client can radically change my workload. And heaven forbid if two of such phone calls come in during the same week or even the same day, as has been known to happen. It feels like being in a car going from zero to sixty in six seconds . . . or sometimes less.

I'd like to be able to give some good advice about how to smooth out your workload so that it's always at a comfortable level—neither too much nor too little but just right. But I haven't managed to do that for myself in close to three decades of freelancing, so I'm not sure I am in a position to hand out coping strategies on this topic. Instead, let's talk about the two challenges— stress and time management—that come with fluctuating workloads, and which, oddly enough, are present both when you're overloaded with work *and* when you have insufficient work.

## All Stressed Out

It's ironic, isn't it, that you may lose sleep when you have too little work *and* when you have too much? Learning to keep this stress under control comes with experience.

The first few times you're seriously overburdened with deadlines may cause a real freak-out. But with time, you'll become more confident in your ability to get it all done. I remember the first time I was working simultaneously on two book manuscripts. I was really stressed and not at all sure I could get them both done by the publishers' deadlines. But I did, and so the next time this happened, I was less stressed because I had already proven to myself that it could be done. (Although, to be honest, after the second time around with this, I vowed never, ever to take on two books at the same time. It falls into the category of "Yeah, I could do that; but I really don't want to.")

When you're overly busy, one solution that helps is to subcontract work to colleagues. In the late 1990s, when I was doing only public relations and event management work, I often had three people at a time working for me as independent contractors. This relieved my stress, enabled me to take on larger clients and projects, and significantly increased my billings. Of course, selecting and managing subcontractors can add a different kind of stress to your business and isn't even a possibility in some fields. But if your profession lends itself to having subcontractors, this method can be a huge stress reliever and an income builder, as long as you choose these people carefully.

Similarly, once you've been through several periods when you wonder whether the phone will ever ring again with new business opportunities, you will learn what you need to do to get things back on track. This will usually involve networking, networking, and, yes, more networking. Of course, if you had been networking steadily all along, you may have been able to avoid having a real slowdown in business. But the natural tendency is to slow or even stop networking activities when business is really good. Despite being a huge believer in networking, I, too, have made this mistake a few times, always to my great regret.

## Too Much or Too Little Time

Time management, like stress, can be challenging both when you're too busy *and*, oddly, when you're not busy enough. Time management is an essential skill for the self-employed. When you're really busy, you have to know how to juggle the demands and deadlines of multiple clients, and this requires knowing how to make the most of every minute. As I already discussed in chapter 4, without some time-management techniques in your tool kit, you will be in danger of working night and day and losing all balance in your life.

The other thing I can suggest is equally difficult to do. When your workload is threatening to overtake your life, learn to just say no. I know . . . it's really hard to turn down business or to ask if you can delay starting a project for a couple of weeks. But sometimes for your sanity and to ensure that you are able to perform at your best, that's a bullet you just have to bite. It took me at least a decade of self-employment before I could bring myself to turn down work. But each time I've done so, things have worked out for the better. Most clients are willing to be reasonable about such things. And if they truly value your services, they'll wait a little while to get them.

The time-management challenge when your workload is scanty is to keep your eye on the ball. This is particularly true if you work at home. It is all too easy for household chores to grab your attention when you're not overly busy with work. You may think that since you're not rushed with work, you can put the projects you do have off until tomorrow. This is a recipe for disaster; more often than not, your phone will ring tomorrow with a client who has a big urgent project, and now you'll be behind the eight ball because you had been procrastinating.

What you need to focus on during slow times is not painting the spare bedroom but rather new business activities that will bring in more work. Seeking new business is the least favorite part of business for many people, so it is all too easy to delay such activities. But if you hope to get out of a slump, this is the only path.

---

### ✐ Other Voices ✐

**Stefan Lindegaard:** Fluctuation impacts flexibility. When you have done this long enough, you get a better sense of the ups and downs and how this will impact your workflow. I prefer to work with paying clients—no wonder—but I always have a long list of things to do that can help me bring in better business opportunities later if there is a slow period. I write lots of blog posts, I visit with prospective clients and relevant contacts, and I try to learn new things and do lots of research. There are always too many things to do as an entrepreneur or as a self-employed person. One of the key challenges is to choose what is the most relevant thing to spend your time on while having both the short-, mid-, and long-term perspectives in mind.

**Barbara Rodriguez:** At times, it seems it's either feast or famine. This is another reason to diversify. Many businesses are seasonal, and you can expect to get work from them at certain times of the year. Our state contracts are busy year-round, although we keep our eyes open for certain local or national news that might require our services, such as the H1N1 virus. Suddenly, many school systems were calling us to translate flyers to send home to parents. Our school customers always scramble prior to the start of classes in September because they need their student handbooks translated and messages ready to send home to parents about the coming year, and, of course, everything is a rush and due yesterday. So when the work comes, we scramble to get it done, and it makes up for the times where work is slow.

When I started the business, I used to worry that I'd get up one morning and none of my customers would call and that everything would just go down the tubes. It never happened. When things get slow, this is your opportunity to find new customers. At some point, you start feeling that the business has taken on a life of its own. If you provide reliable quality services, word can't help but get around. Our best customers have been referred by other long-time customers. At some point you get to play off of what you already have. Say I'm going after another school customer. I let them know all the schools that we have been doing business with and how satisfied they are. I provide them with contact names, people they can call who are in the same business who can attest to our good service and quality.

**Howie Green:** I have found that consistently mid-July to mid-August are always the slowest weeks of the year. Then mid-August all hell breaks loose. I chalk this up to vacations and bad planning on my clients' part. They always push everything in the third quarter off until August, then panic and go crazy to get all their projects completed by Labor Day. And it doesn't seem to matter what kind of business they're in; the August panic is tried and true.

# CHAPTER TWELVE

# Clients Who Don't Hold Up Their End of the Bargain

Some years ago, a client who is also a long-time friend sent me an e-mail asking for advice about how to handle an awkward situation. Ten days earlier, a new client of hers had signed a contract that stipulated that a down payment on my friend's work was due upon the signing of the contract. However, the client didn't bring a check with her and instead said it would be coming "in a few days."

Now, the client was sending my friend e-mails pushing her to begin the work they had agreed on, despite the fact that no check had arrived yet. When my friend asked about the payment, the client wrote back that because their company was very small, their bookkeeper was a part-timer and thus the check hadn't been written yet. She said my friend's invoice was "on the top of the pile" for when the bookkeeper did come in to work later that week.

My friend wanted my opinion on whether she should just go ahead and begin the work even though the client had not lived up to her side of their written agreement.

Anyone who is self-employed can share a similar story. People sign contracts and then renege on one of the terms of the agreement. But in our desire to get a new relationship off to a good start, we often let this slide, which is what my friend was considering doing.

In my response to her, I suggested she not do that. I told her to stick by her guns about the upfront payment. I said, "We both know that if this CEO wants to get a check written, she can get it written today."

My friend is a CPA, and although her practice now is not in the financial realm, she knew what I was saying was true even better than I did. So she wrote to the client and told her the contract stipulation that the first payment be made before work started was based on her experience in being burned by several nonprofits and start-ups in the past. And thus she was going to have to enforce the requirement in the contract the client had signed.

The client replied, "Ouch . . . okay, now I understand," and the check was mailed immediately! My friend felt empowered, and I was glad I was there to help her see her way through a difficult situation.

## The Takeaway

Here's the lesson to take from this example: If in your desire to make a new client happy, you let that client walk all over you for no good reason, prepare yourself for more of the same as the relationship unfolds. Recognize that some clients have control issues; they like to be the one in charge, and this can express itself in the type of behavior my friend's new client exhibited.

In this case, the client's need to get a project started was *all* that mattered to her. The commitment she had made in the signed contract was a minor detail to her. Thus, she fed my friend the blarney about the bookkeeper. It wasn't that she didn't intend to eventually pay my friend; it's just that doing so was not high on her priority list until my friend stood her ground.

## Coping Strategies

- **Set clear expectations at the outset.** When you're working with first-time clients, this involves getting a signed contract that stipulates what both you and your new client expect of each other. This should cover deliverables, due dates, who is responsible for doing what, pricing and payment information, as well as any other information that is normal for your field to include in a contract. For example, when I ghostwrite a book, my contract stipulates that the person who is hiring me owns the copyright for the completed work. In those cases where I am to be included as a coauthor, the contract stipulates that my name will be on the book cover and title page.

    Industry groups can give you guidance on what needs to be included in a contract. Of course, you'll probably end up using a variety of contracts to fit each particular situation. If I'm hired to perform a small job, I often just put together a one-page proposal that outlines all the pertinent information on the work to be done, deadlines, and payment.

For a more involved project, such as ghostwriting a book, I use a much more detailed contract that follows recommended industry guidelines.

- **Embrace your power.** Too many times, people who are self-employed don't realize the power they hold in client relationships. In their desire to hold onto business, they back down when push comes to shove. It has always been my belief that in the long run, you won't succeed—and you certainly won't be very happy—if you turn yourself into a doormat. In the example above, by setting a firm tone at the outset, my friend stood a far better chance of having this relationship be one in which she would be respected instead of walked on.
- **Recognize when compromise is needed.** If you're going to build long-term client relationships based on mutual respect and trust, you will find times when you need to compromise. Clients often have an understandable explanation for why they aren't living up to a commitment they've made to you.
- **Rely on clear and open communications to sort things out.** Discuss problems that arise openly and honestly, making it clear what the client's failure to meet the conditions set forth in your initial agreement means to the future of the project.

For instance, if a client is not meeting their own deadlines for getting approvals back to you so that you can move forward to the next project phase, present them with a revised schedule that shows the impact their delays will have on the project's completion date. Sure, you might be able to make up some time and keep things on track, but you can't be expected to overcome repeated delays and still complete the project by the deadline you both agreed to at the start. Again, this is about taking the power that you have instead of just folding like a house of cards when faced with clients who are not living up to their end of the bargain.

Clients who are reneging on financial commitments are clearly tricky and require a whole different set of coping skills. Refer to the chapter on deadbeat clients in part III for advice on how to handle such situations.

# CHAPTER THIRTEEN

# Handling Competing Client Crises

Some months ago, I arrived at my desk one morning to find that two clients both had projects that were on fire. By this I mean they both needed my *immediate* help composing important communications—one to employees and the other to the press. While I had known that the events that precipitated these needs were in the offing, there had been no way to predict that they would occur simultaneously.

This is not the first time—and likely won't be the last—that I've faced competing client crises. Anyone who has been self-employed for any length of time is bound to run into such situations. Your stress level immediately soars as you try to plot out the best plan of attack because the very last thing you ever want to do is disappoint a client at a time when they are counting on you to come through for them in an important situation.

These questions go through your mind: Is it possible to get both things done in the time frame allotted? How should I prioritize the work? Might I need to call on a colleague for assistance? If so, what's the best way to divide up the work? And, of course, you have to consider whether the crisis is for real . . . or is the client just being overly demanding and creating a crisis when one really doesn't exist, which happens more often than you'd think.

In the particular situation I faced, neither client was being unreasonable. One client really did have *major* company news to share with employees and needed to have a message written up in time to get photocopied and stuffed in the payroll envelopes that would be given out the following morning. And the other client, a nonprofit, had promised to issue a press release by noon to coincide with a big announcement coming from the White House. Yes, *that* White House, the one at 1600 Pennsylvania Avenue in Washington! Believe me, opportunities to toss the White House into the headline of your press release don't come along every day, so you want to take advantage of it when you can!

Fortunately, in this instance I was well prepared to complete these projects, having done significant prep work already. Both jobs got done on time, and my blood pressure returned to normal levels.

## Uncontrollable Outside Forces

But there have been times when competing client crises have occurred that weren't so readily resolved. Often this happens when a crisis is caused from uncontrollable forces outside a client's organization, so they (and you) have absolutely no heads-up in advance that something big is about to occur. For example, one of my former clients was a small community savings bank; several times during the five or so years that I handled their public relations, I got phone calls about branch robberies that had just occurred. At these times, they needed a press statement made ready immediately. One of these calls came when I was in the midst of a crisis for another client. Major juggling ensued.

If you're the type of person who is easily rattled by having to deal with one crisis, let alone two, this is something you should consider before making the leap into self-employment. If you're used to working in the corporate world, this may be a totally new situation for you since in big companies you usually can rely on having a team of people who can jump in to help at such times. This leads to the first of the coping strategies below.

## Coping Strategies

- **Have backup help, if possible.** When you're a solopreneur, handling multiple crises simultaneously is very challenging. Consider developing a relationship with someone else in a similar position so that you can rely on each other for help in such situations. Carol Savage, one of the Other Voices you read in this book, and I have been each other's backstop for decades now. We're each there for the other when one of us is feeling overwhelmed by a client crisis or by competing client crises.
- **Learn to tell a fake crisis from the real thing.** It is important to recognize that not everything that a client claims is a crisis is an actual

emergency. Yes, some events, such as the robberies at my client's bank branches, do require immediate action. But I've also had clients call who were all in a panic about a crisis that was an emergency only in their heads. Be sure you understand the realities of the situation before you decide to give one situation priority over another.

For example, I've had more than one client call and say they suddenly want work delivered ASAP that wasn't due for several days. Further discussion reveals that this so-called crisis is being caused by the fact that they've decided to go out of town for a few days and they'd like to be able to read whatever project we're working on while they're on the plane. Their need for reading material for a plane trip does not mean I should drop everything I'm doing and get their work done days early, something I have had to gently but firmly convey to them.

No doubt you'll run into your own version of fake crises. As you get to know clients better, you will soon learn who is apt to cry wolf over nothing and who only labels something a crisis that actually is a crisis. Personally, after several fake emergencies, I am always tempted to fire the client who repeatedly cries wolf.

- **Be sure you always have good ongoing client communication, which will help prepare you for crises.** As mentioned regarding the double crisis situation I talked about earlier in this chapter, it helped me greatly that I had already done significant prep work for the two clients involved. This was possible because I try to maintain a good flow of communication with clients so that I know what's coming up on their agendas. With one of these clients, I participated in weekly marketing conference calls, which were hugely helpful in enabling me to anticipate their upcoming needs.

  Will you sometimes be caught completely unaware by a client crisis? Sure, but if you work to stay in touch to the degree possible without making yourself an annoyance, you're more likely to be kept in the loop and will then be prepared to respond well.

- **Stay calm when under fire.** Be prepared to react effectively when clients are competing for your time. It isn't always a crisis; sometimes it is just people wanting 100 percent of your attention and not being willing to acknowledge that they are not your only client. Working out how to juggle these kinds of demands is a huge part of being successful at self-employment. Keeping everyone happy without suffering from burnout or so much stress that it affects your well-being is your goal.

## ℐ Other Voices ℐ

**Howie Green:** My clients don't want to know that I have other clients. They are the only ones. So I never, ever mention other clients. If time crunches happen, I tend to use family or personal reasons for rearranging my schedule because clients understand those kinds of demands.

# CHAPTER FOURTEEN

# Sudden, Unexpected
# Client Defections

During the Great Recession, I lost two clients that I had been working with for several years. One was a business incubator whose funding came from the state; when tax revenues plummeted, they had to stop publishing the quarterly newsletter I had been writing for them for the past three years. The other client was an investment banking firm; when the mergers and acquisitions market dried up in 2008, they could no longer afford to have me write their press releases or the monthly white papers we had started four years earlier. Given the economic mess the country was in, both of these developments were foreseeable and I wasn't surprised at all when I got the news.

All self-employed individuals, however, experience client defections that come out of left field. In my line of work, a new marketing director will come in and decide to clean house, replacing current freelancers with ones he/she has worked with in the past or perhaps building their staff so that the work can be done in-house. Or a client may decide they "need to take things in a new direction"—one of the most disheartening phrases a freelancer can hear. Aside from whatever else it may mean, the bottom line is that you're out and someone else is in.

Such things are part and parcel of the self-employed life. I count myself lucky that I've faced relatively few such surprises. In fact, in several instances I outlasted new marketing directors who vowed to shake things up and was still around long after the new faces had left the building. I always took pride in having long-term relationships with clients, and, indeed, I've had clients with whom I've worked for well over a decade, a lifetime in my line of work.

## A Blow out of Left Field

That's why a completely unexpected defection came as such a jolt to me in 2011. My oldest client—a company I had worked with literally from the first day I began my business in 1989—decided in January of 2011 to ban the use of freelancers. This was not an unreasonable decision given how hard it was for them to drum up new business in an economy that was still struggling. Better to stop using freelancers than lay off staff. But guess what? They didn't tell me for months!

Not having assignments from this client for two or three months in a row was not unusual; such a lull would then usually be followed by a flurry of work over several months. So I didn't think anything of it when I didn't hear from them in January, February, or March. Although the work was sometimes sporadic, I had been able to rely on this client for thousands of dollars of business each year—through good times and bad—for over two decades.

In April, the company's owner and I had one of our periodic dinners, and she casually revealed the no freelancer decision that had been made by the employee she had promoted to COO in January. Gosh, I thought, it would have been nice to get some advance notice so that I would know I needed to gear up the new business machine to replace this significant piece of my business. As it turned out, I *was* able to replace their business, but by the time the news reached me that I needed to do so, I had wasted several months, during which I should have been seeking new clients.

The lesson here is that if you're going to be self-employed, you need to be aware that no matter how close you've been to their organization or how long you've worked together, clients often do not consider the impact of their decisions on you or take you into their confidence when making decisions that negatively affect you. In short, you may feel like you're part of the family, but you're really not. Never take anything for granted when you're self-employed. Just because a company has hired you consistently for twenty-one years doesn't mean they'll be there for you in year twenty-two.

## Coping Strategies

- **Keep your ear to the ground for rumblings of client financial problems.** Pay close attention to what is happening with your clients' businesses. Even in good economic times, some companies struggle. Once, a retail company that my colleague Carol Savage and I were doing public relations for declared bankruptcy. For many freelancers this would have been bad news, especially if it left you hanging with an unpaid invoice or two. In the short-term, this development actually meant more work for us because a lot of PR and employee communications needed to be done surrounding the bankruptcy, and this was an expense allowed by the bankruptcy judge. So while we did eventually lose the client, we didn't lose money and actually had a bump in our billings during the bankruptcy.

We were fortunate, but that certainly is not the case with all self-employed people who are performing work for or selling goods to a company that goes belly up. The last thing you want to do is to become just another unsecured creditor in a bankruptcy case, so always be alert for signals that all might not be well financially with your clients. If you get an inkling that the company is on shaky financial ground, you have two choices:

1) Have a heart-to-heart talk with your client and see if you can come up with a way to protect your financial interests while continuing to service the client. For instance, when a client I'd worked with off and on for some time suddenly started paying my invoices thirty or more days late, we shifted to a flat-fee-paid-in-advance approach that served us both better. I no longer had to make nagging phone calls asking for payment, and they no longer had to make excuses about why they hadn't paid as promised. We both felt better.

This new approach, of course, required that I be able to calculate the hours a project would require in order to set a flat fee that would be paid in advance. The risk here was that I would underestimate the hours needed, but as far as I was concerned, this was offset by the benefit of having the money paid up front rather than waiting sixty to ninety days for it. Plus, the fact is that if you've been doing something for a good while, as I have, you are probably pretty good at figuring out the required hours.

2) Wind down your involvement with the client and find replacement income. Sometimes the handwriting on the wall becomes so clear that you're better off getting out while the getting is good. I realize this may be easier said than done depending on your line of work and how involved you are with the client's operation. Your odds of walking away with all that you are owed depends greatly on the client's ethics, their actual ability to pay, and how dogged you wish to be in collecting.

- **Also, be alert for signs of other imminent changes that may affect your business with the client.** Financial difficulties are not the only reason behind unexpected client defections. As I mentioned earlier, a new executive may be hired who wants to shake things up by bringing in new vendors. Or, as was the case with one of my longest-running clients, the client may decide on a lifestyle change that means they'll be cutting back in some areas of their business. In my case, the client ran a consulting firm and wanted to scale back her involvement so that she could devote time to her growing interest in painting. She brought on a younger partner in the hope that this person would take over the marketing, which included managing my work. For a number of reasons, this plan didn't work out, and they eventually stopped the marketing activities in which I had been involved for well over a decade.

Because I was well aware of the founder's desire to slow down and of the issues she subsequently was having with getting the new partner to pick up the slack, this was not exactly an unexpected defection, but it is just one more example of the wide variety of reasons why you might lose a client even after years of working together. When clients start talking about their desire for change, listen carefully for signs that this desire is turning into a reality that might affect your business relationship with them.

- **Bear in mind that clients won't tell you everything.** Because of the nature of my work, clients do tend to tell me more than they perhaps do other vendors. After all, I am the one who has to write the press releases when big news—good or bad—occurs. However, this doesn't mean that I've always had an inside track on big developments, such as the sale of the company. And neither will you. When a sale is pending, most company owners will keep it very close to the vest, with very few people in the know. So you may be blindsided from time to time by big news like this. Not that all sales mean you're going to be out of the picture, because you may be able to make a connection with the new owner and continue on with the relationship. Just don't plan on this happening.

## ✐ Other Voices ✐

**Stefan Lindegaard:** Keep developing your abilities and stay sharp so that you can apply your skills in different ways. Here is where the idea of thinking in terms of intersections could work (see Stefan's comments in chapter 8). If possible, work in different world regions. If some are down, others seem to do better.

**Barbara Rodriguez:** Some businesses do better in a bad economy. That was the case with our business when the economy soured in

2008, and it was directly related to working with state agencies. In a bad economy, more people apply for services such as unemployment, so we provided interpreters for unemployment hearings. The same with disability applications, which also tend to increase in bad economic times; we provided interpreters for disability evaluations with doctors and psychiatrists.

**Howie Green:** One of the realities of my world is that clients come and go like a revolving door. Some stick around for one project and some for years, so you always need to be prospecting for new clients . . . always.

**Pat Mullaly:** Once in a great while I've had a client with whom I've worked for years suddenly find a new designer. It's happened when there was a change in top personnel. My contact at a company was leaving for a similar position in a new company. Knowing their replacement was likely to bring in his/her own people, I asked for a meeting so that I could be introduced to the new person and make my pitch. I also let my contact know how much I enjoyed working with them and would appreciate any work from their new company. Then I started looking for a new client.

# CHAPTER FIFTEEN

# When Vendors Let You Down

Many of us who are self-employed routinely are involved with other vendors who are needed to complete various aspects of client projects. Sometimes these vendors are people we recommend to our client, who then pays the vendor directly. Other times, you may bring in these vendors as part of your team; their work is included in your invoices, and you then pay them once you are paid. Or you may end up working with a vendor you know nothing about who has been hired directly by the client. No matter what the scenario, if a vendor delivers subpar work for a project you are managing, you may be in for a world of hurt.

For instance, I frequently recommend graphic designers to my clients. Those designers in turn hire printers to complete print projects we've worked on together. Having recommended someone or hired them on behalf of your client, if they don't perform up to standards, it is your reputation and your relationship with the client that is on the line. In some cases, you may even be financially liable if a vendor does not perform well. This makes it very important to carefully vet any vendor you recommend or hire to work on a project.

I make it a practice to work only with vendors I've known for a long time or who come highly recommended by a very trusted colleague. I have usually ended up regretting it the few times I've veered from this policy, so the longer I've been in business, the harder it has become for a new-to-me vendor to get added to the list of people I recommend or hire on behalf of a client.

## Be Wary of Low-Priced Bidders

Once in a while, you may have to hire someone who works in a field in which you don't have trusted vendors. In such cases, it can be tempting to solicit bids from vendors and then just go with the lowest price. Before doing so, I recommend doing some homework first, such as getting references for each vendor from several of their clients. To lessen the chance of having problems later on, I urge you to put far more emphasis on these reference checks than you do on pricing. Sure, you want to save your clients money if you can, but if it comes at the expense of good work, it won't be worth the savings . . . nor the damage it will do to your client relationship if you bring in someone who can't deliver good work.

Here's an example of why I urge you to rely more on references than on pricing when hiring vendors for your client. Several years ago, I served on a chamber of commerce committee that sought to hire a new printer for its newsletter. I volunteered to get cost proposals from three printers that belonged to the chamber and to call two or three customers for each vendor to check out their performance. One printing company got some of the most glowing references I had ever heard, but its price was not the lowest. Lo and behold, the chamber director decided to go against the committee's advice and hired the lowest bidder, despite the fact that the clients of this printer with whom I spoke had given *very* lukewarm endorsements. The director soon reported problems with the new printer delivering the newsletter on time. Maybe she was shocked, but I sure wasn't.

In this instance, I was very glad this hadn't been one of my clients who opted for the low-cost option and ignored negative information on the printer's work quality and ability to meet deadlines. But I have had cases in which a client insisted on using a vendor that I thought might not be up to doing the job. Also, you may find yourself working with subpar vendors who have a preexisting relationship with the client. If either of these situations comes your way, I hope the coping strategies below will be of help.

## Coping Strategies

- **Carefully document problems with vendors.** This is especially important if you're working with a vendor you don't know but who has a long-standing relationship with your client. At some point, you may need this documentation to track the project's progress in case there is a problem. Or the documentation will support your recommendation that the client should seek a new vendor for future projects.

- **Do not take it for granted that a vendor you've worked with previously will always do a great job.** It's important to stay informed of the progress a vendor is making on a project you're working on together and to speak up quickly if something seems to be going awry. This is particularly important if it is a vendor you've brought onto the job. After all, it is your reputation on the line just as much as theirs.

  A few years ago, a graphic designer and I were working on a project for a mutual friend who had worked with both of us off and on for over twenty years. In this case, the designer had begun work on the project before I was brought on board, and so I was not guiding her work. Much to the surprise of the client and me, it soon became clear that the designer was making errors that were seriously delaying the project.

  Because the relationship with the designer had been so long and so positive previously, the client delayed talking to the designer about her concerns until the list of problems had gotten very long. The main lesson to be learned from this example is this: When a vendor relationship starts to go off the tracks, it is best to find out why ASAP and to then take the business elsewhere if a solution isn't apparent. This is true whether the client is responsible for hiring the vendor or you are.

- **Make the best of a bad situation if you must work with a vendor you don't respect.** There may come a time when a client chooses to pair you with a vendor that you think isn't the best choice. Clients choose vendors for many reasons that aren't related to their capabilities; for instance, I once had to work with a very inexperienced website designer who happened to be the nephew of my client. The ink was barely dry on the kid's high school diploma, for heaven's sakes! All I could do was grit my teeth and try to move the project forward.

  It's important to understand that clients often have no real idea of what qualifications a vendor should have for a particular job, so they go with a friend or relative because that feels comfortable to them. If this decision is made without your input, you must live with the consequences, which often include having to try as best you can to steer the vendor in the right direction. And, of course, apply the first coping strategy above in case an opportunity does present itself down the road to recommend a different, better vendor to your client.

- **Consider whether professional liability insurance is worth your while.** Commonly referred to as errors and omissions insurance, this type of insurance protects service providers from mistakes that harm a client financially. There are special policies written for a wide variety of industries. Check to see what type of insurance is available for your particular field and assess whether you might need such coverage.

What you need to determine is how much risk is really involved in what you're doing in comparison to the cost of the insurance. If something goes wrong on a project involving multiple vendors, such as a copywriter, a graphic designer, and a printer, the client may want to reach into the pocket of everyone involved for reimbursement, regardless of whether it was you who was actually involved in causing the error. Having insurance at such times would be a big help.

## ✐ Other Voices ✐

**Howie Green:** After years of having vendors screw up jobs and cost me money, I started demanding that my clients use their own vendors. Every one of them preferred to do that, which was a huge relief. They save money, and they are responsible for the vendor relationship, not me.

**Pat Mullaly:** I've been very lucky to work with some wonderful vendors. There have been a few losers in the bunch, but most have done great work. Depending on the project, I often recommend qualified vendors. But if a client wants to use someone of their own choosing, it's no problem. I make it clear the responsibility for the decision is theirs. I do my best to work with the vendor. But if things go south, it's not on my head.

CHAPTER SIXTEEN

# Self-Employment Lessons
# I Learned from My Father

All this talk about issues that can arise with clients can be stress inducing, so let's relax a bit and take a trip down memory lane . . . my memory lane, that is. I grew up with a model of self-employment right in my own home from my earliest days. My father operated a small sawmill in Pennsylvania. He managed to survive without any business training beyond having watched his own dad, who also ran a sawmill. My father did this in an industry that was often hard hit by economic downturns and in which snow-filled winters forced him to shut down for months at a time.

From our little out-of-the-way rural location in south central Pennsylvania, he developed a diversified clientele, selling lumber to everybody from the Pennsylvania Railroad, which needed a steady stream of railroad ties, to Amish buggy makers in Lancaster County (who were *very* particular about their lumber, by the way; they bought only the highest grade), to local people who needed a dump truck load of wood to heat their homes through the winter.

Since my father conducted the business end of his operation from our home, I frequently heard him on the phone negotiating a deal either to sell lumber or to buy his next stand of timber. And when I was in my early teens, he started having me write out the payroll checks each Friday. Both of these were good exposure to the intricacies of being your own boss.

Here are my takeaways from watching him operate that have served me well while operating my own business.

- **Do something you love.** The work my father did was dirty, hard, and dangerous. According to the Bureau of Labor Statistics, logging is the second most dangerous occupation in America. (Fishing is the most dangerous job.) With his well-being and that of his workers on the line out there in the woods every day, it was a good thing he loved what he did.

  Even as a kid, I could tell how much Dad loved being out in the woods and cherished finding good timber to buy. Cherry was his favorite wood, and you could see the excitement in his face when he got his hands on furniture-grade cherry logs. I had friends whose fathers had nine-to-five types of jobs that you could tell didn't excite them. Even as a child, I could tell there was a difference between my father's passion for his work and what my pals' dads were doing to earn a living. I feel fortunate to have a skill—writing—that I feel equally passionate about that has enabled me to be my own boss and earn a decent living.

- **Do the right thing.** If you wanted to see smoke come out of my father's ears, all you had to do was say the words "clear-cutting." This method of taking down nearly every tree on the side of a mountain was an anathema to him. I received a "lecture" on the topic any time we drove past a site where some big lumber company had clear-cut a patch of mountain land. He believed that cutting down only mature trees and leaving the younger trees with room to grow was far better for the long-term health of the ecosystem (although certainly Dad never used a fancy word like ecosystem!).

  The lesson I took from this was that there was a right way to go about doing business and a wrong way. And if I'm ever tempted to take a short cut (no pun intended), all I have to do is remember Dad's rants against the clear-cutters.

- **Treat your small customers just as well as you treat the big ones.** Whether someone was coming to Dad to buy a few boards to fix their back steps or they were in the market for truckloads of lumber, my father treated everyone the same. He didn't kowtow to the big guys, and he didn't act like the small folks' business wasn't important to him. This is an attitude that I've practiced throughout my career, and it has served me well. I've had small clients turn into big ones, and they've stuck with me even though they could afford to go with a larger firm.

- **Diversify, diversify, diversify.** As I mentioned, my father sold his lumber to a wide variety of people in many different industries. This certainly helped him weather the ups and downs of the lumber market, which depends on many different factors. For example, although he did not sell to the housing industry, when the housing market tanked, all lumber prices would plummet.

What I took from this was to not depend on any one industry for your livelihood. I have seen other people in my field cluster their clients in one industry only to face dire straits when that industry collapsed. Think real estate or the dot-com bubble of the late 1990s. I'm glad my father taught me better.

These are just of a few of the business lessons I learned by observing my father. He passed away two years before I started my own business. But I know he would be proud that the lessons I learned from observing him have helped me survive for more than twenty-eight years of self-employment.

### ✐ Other Voices ✐

**Howie Green:** My dad was a sales guy and always had a home office. Since we only had one phone, when it rang it was often one of his clients, so we were raised from babies that you do not, under any circumstances, goof around on the phone. When you answer, be polite and professional. Speak clearly and take messages. Great advice for phone or e-mail behavior. You never know who could be calling.

# PART III

# FINANCIAL EXPECTATIONS

# CHAPTER SEVENTEEN

# Being Financially Self-Sufficient

My self-employed friends are about equally divided between those who are married and those who are single. When tough economic times hit, as they did in the Great Recession, I worry a lot more about the single ones than the married ones because being single and self-employed means that, financially speaking, you're out there on the high wire without a net. (Unless, of course, you've had the good fortune of being a trust-fund baby.) If your business starts to fall off, you better hope you've managed to stash away plenty of savings or that things turn around pronto—and that you haven't already maxed out your credit cards. I got married for the first time just three years ago, so I know exactly how hard and how scary it can be to be totally on your own financially.

This may sound harsh, but when one of my self-employed friends who is part of a two-income household frets about his/her business being slow or a client not paying on time, I say all the appropriate commiserating things, all the while thinking, "You think you're worried now? Try being totally on your own financially speaking and see how worried you get when those unpaid bills stack up."

## Is This Really for You?

The reality is that being single and self-employed means you don't have a financial fallback, a situation that definitely isn't for everyone. If you fret about money a lot, even when you have a steady, secure job, the stress over finances you'll experience when self-employed is likely to be considerably greater. For this reason, I caution any single person who is thinking of making the leap from employee to self-employment to consider the financial implications carefully.

Of course, no job is totally secure in today's economy, but at least if you get laid off, you can collect unemployment. If an unmarried self-employed person's business takes a nose dive, no government program is going to lend them a hand (unless, heaven forbid, they get to the point where they qualify for food stamps).

None of this, of course, is to say that married people who are self-employed are immune to concerns about money. They, too, have their share of bills to pay and can be beset by worry if their business starts to slide. This means they, too, have to think about how much financial pressure they can handle before deciding to go into business on their own.

The advice I have to offer you here is less about coping strategies and more in the way of advice of what you need to consider before making the decision to quit your day job and try to go it on your own, especially if you are single and have no financial Plan B.

- **Build up your financial reserves first.** It takes time to build a successful business and the income that comes with it. If feasible, moonlight for a while and set that income aside to help you when you're out on your own.
- **Make sure you've done all your homework in terms of fully understanding how long it will take you to build up a clientele.** Now is not the time to be wearing rose-colored glasses, that's for sure. Be realistic; test your idea with advisers and mentors you truly trust.
- **Know the market rates for what you're offering.** If you're going to be offering a service, thoroughly research what the going rates are for that service. Calculate how many billable hours you're likely to have per week and then see how the resulting income matches with what you need to pay your bills. Be conservative in your estimates of how many billable hours you're likely to have for the first year or two of your business. Recognize that you'll have to spend a significant amount of time on nonbillable duties, such as finding prospective customers and perhaps writing proposals, to name only some time-consuming activities. Any estimate that has you billing the major portion of your day, especially early on, is probably out of whack.

  In your calculations of needed income, don't overlook the fact that once you're self-employed, you will be paying the full freight in Social

Security and Medicare taxes. This is a killer. Even after close to thirty years of self-employment, I am still shocked every year when I look at the line on my tax form that represents what I'm paying in terms of the self-employment tax. (See more on this in chapter 19.)

Again, I'm not saying you should not give being your own boss a shot if you're single. Many, many single people do fine without a financial backstop. Before I married in 2015, I made it through twenty-seven years and three recessions and always paid the mortgage on time. But I am pointing out the things that might trip you up if you don't plan carefully and realistically. My hope is that by having this information, you'll make the decision that is right for you.

---

### ✐ Other Voices ✐

**Howie Green:** Well, I'm an artist, so financial stability has always been an elusive dream and one I was never that freaked out about—besides, I always have my trusty accountant at my side just a screaming phone call away.

# CHAPTER EIGHTEEN

# Saving for Retirement

Poll after poll shows that a high portion of baby boomers have little or no faith they'll have enough money to retire when their careers end. Most experts believe they have a right to be worried. For one group of baby boomers—the self-employed—accumulating retirement savings is particularly challenging. When you're out here on your own, nobody but you is contributing to your retirement nest egg.

I have spent over half my career working for myself. When you're self-employed, you pay the full freight on Social Security and Medicare taxes. No doubt Social Security will be a key part of your retirement income. But paying the full tax yourself, instead of having an employer pay half for you, leaves you with less income—at current tax rates just under 8 percent less—to invest in IRAs and other retirement accounts, many of which will hopefully earn more than your "investment" in Social Security does. That's a significant amount of money year in and year out. This difference alone adds up over the decades, believe me. Also, no employer is contributing to a 401K for you.

This can be extremely challenging, especially in years when your income is down due to a poor economy or any one of the many other factors that can cause your income to fluctuate from year to year. Financial experts—many of whom, no doubt, are safely employed by someone and aren't paying their own full Social Security tax—always advise making saving for retirement your highest priority. They tell you that the first thing you should do with every client check that comes in is *first* set part of it aside for retirement. Talk about a classic case of "easier said than done."

I don't know anyone who is self-employed who doesn't have cash flow ups and downs. And, naturally, when it comes to deciding whether to pay the mortgage or sending money to your IRA, guess which choice most people make? We always think, "Oh, well, I can make up that IRA payment next month." But then next month comes and more tough choices need to be made.

## Second Guessing One's Choices

The amount of discipline required to get this right is enormous. Some days I wonder if I made the right choice. Wouldn't I have been better off working for someone else . . . perhaps one of the large corporations I used to work for? According to most studies, I have saved over three times more for retirement than the average for my age group, but that is far from comforting given how shockingly low and inadequate the average amount of savings is. And even though I'm better off than many people, my retirement savings are nowhere near the amount the experts say you should have socked away.

In the 1970s, I worked for a major life insurance company for nearly eight years and was partially vested in their pension plan when I left. When I reached sixty-five, they began sending me a pension check for $78.82 each month. I sometimes reflect on how much bigger that check would be if I had stayed there for a few more decades. My best friend at that company was hired just a month or two before I was. She retired a couple years ago after spending more than thirty years there. I imagine she has absolutely no worries about having enough income for her retirement years.

Yet I also recall, as I mentioned early in this book, that other friends in Boston spent decades with Polaroid only to have the money they had saved for retirement in the employee stock ownership plan made worthless when the company went bankrupt in 2001. Starting over again at age fifty or so, as some of these people had to do, must have been enormously scary. It's stories like those that show what a crapshoot the whole thing is. Who, after all, would have predicted that a company like Polaroid would go broke and leave its employees high and dry? So when I reflect on that, it makes me glad that at least my fate is more or less in my own hands.

## Coping Strategies

- **Get good advice regarding the retirement account options available to the self-employed.** The good news is that you have options beyond a traditional IRA or a Roth IRA. For example, you can set up what is called a simplified employee pension, or SEP, which will allow you to contribute 25 percent of your net earnings up to a limit that is periodically adjusted by the IRS. Deciding which type of accounts—or which combination of accounts, since you can have several at the same time—is something I'd urge you to discuss with an experienced financial planner.

A financial planner can also create a plan to set a retirement savings goal and tell you how much you need to put aside each month to achieve that goal. This can be a great motivator because without having such a goal in mind, you may underestimate or overestimate what you need to save.

- **Start saving as early as possible.** The sooner you start saving once you become self-employed, the easier it is to develop the habit and the better off you'll be when retirement time rolls around. This is especially true if you begin self-employment early in your working years. Even a small amount of money set aside each month beginning in your twenties and thirties can add up to a cozy nest egg by the time retirement rolls around.

- **Delay taking Social Security for as long as you can.** It may be tempting to sign up to receive Social Security at the earliest possible time (currently, age sixty-two), but this is foolish unless you have no other financial option. For each year you delay taking payments past age sixty-two, the amount you will receive goes up between 7 and 8 percent. At the very least, try to hold on until you reach the age at which you can receive your full Social Security benefit; for me that was age sixty-six. And if you work beyond that age and can manage without Social Security, your benefit will continue to rise each year until you reach age seventy.

  Many advisers think it is smarter to tap into an IRA or other savings rather than take Social Security before you absolutely have to because it's hard to beat a 7–8 percent guaranteed investment return. The numbers really do tell the story. A typical senior who would receive $1,350 a month from Social Security at age sixty-two would see that check grow to $2,376 a month if they delayed taking the benefit until age seventy.

- **Work longer . . . or at least work part-time.** In an ideal world, we'd all be able to sock away a ton of money to set us up to retire when we want to. But reality works differently. If you'd asked me when I started self-employment whether I'd still be at it late into my sixties, I would have said no, definitely not. Yet here I am, working on a *greatly* reduced schedule and with only a couple clients, but still working nonetheless.

The best way to look at this is to consider that one of the beautiful things about self-employment is that no one is going to put you out to pasture until you want to go. As long as you can and want to work and can find clients to pay you, you can continue to earn money as long as you wish.

As your own boss, you have a great ability to bring in income that allows you to either avoid dipping into your retirement savings or to delay taking Social Security to maximize your benefit. And, of course, you can work as little or as much as you like, something that is rarely possible if you had an employer. Plus, what I've found so far is that keeping active with work has dividends of its own. It keeps me in touch with clients and colleagues who I enjoy, and it provides intellectual stimulation, which is never a bad thing as you age.

## ✐ Other Voices ✐

**Stefan Lindegaard:** Who needs to save up for retirement? Not me. I will make enough money in my later years, and I will work into my seventies and thus be able to live well for the rest of my life. Ambitions and dreams are good, but sometimes a reality check is what is really needed.

**Howie Green:** Retirement? What's that? I do what I love, and even if I were "retired," I would still be working at what I do. So yeah, I'll be working 'til they get the shovels. I had a retirement plan IRA and a stock portfolio and all those things one is supposed to have and was well on my way to a financially comfortable old age . . . then the stock market crash and recession of 2000–2001 happened and then 2008 happened and yeah . . . I'll just keep working, thanks.

# CHAPTER NINETEEN

# The Taxman Cometh

No book on how to succeed at self-employment would be complete without a chapter about the tax-related challenges posed by being self-employed. Tax-wise, life changes dramatically when you become your own boss. First, there is the agony of having to make quarterly estimated tax payments. And then there is the dreaded self-employment tax, which kills me every year.

The quarterly payments can be challenging. Instead of your employer withholding taxes from each paycheck, you are now responsible for estimating what your income will be for the year and how much tax you will owe, including Social Security and Medicare taxes. Then you have to make quarterly payments toward that tax on April 15, June 15, September 15, and January 15. If you live in a state with a state income tax, you also have to make quarterly estimated payments for that.

Sounds simple enough until you actually have to do it! I don't know about all businesses, but in my line of work it is difficult to know with any degree of certainty on April 15, June 15, or even September 15 what my income may be for the year. Fluctuations can be significant from year to year. And if the year starts off slowly or expenses are up for some reason, coming up with the scratch to make that first estimated quarterly payment on April 15, as well as pay anything you still might owe on your taxes from the prior year on that same date, can be rough.

If you don't pay in enough through your estimated payments, fines and interest will be charged. Making your quarterly payments and getting them in the right amounts is a challenge that many self-employed people fail to master, and thus, they end up in trouble with the IRS. If you're not a disciplined person when it comes to financial matters, consider this carefully before jumping into self-employment.

## The Real Killer

The self-employment tax comes as a serious shock to people who haven't thought through the full financial implications of being out on their own without an employer. Because no employer is paying half of your Social Security and Medicare taxes, you must pay the entire amount. I know . . . gasp!

Each year when I look at my tax return, it is this figure—the self-employment tax—that causes me to groan, not the actual income tax figure. Think about that the next time you look at your pay stub. Check out the FICA number and double it. Does that make you panic a little knowing that if you were self-employed, this would be the amount you'd pay? Now you know how those of us who are self-employed feel each year at tax time—and how you'll feel if you pursue self-employment.

## Coping Strategies

- **When starting out, find a tax pro skilled at working with the self-employed.** When I was working for someone else, I always did my own taxes, because it was a relatively simple matter. But all that changed when I became self-employed. I quickly found that hiring a tax professional who was well-informed on allowable deductions, tax law changes, and similar matters was critical to my peace of mind and well worth the expense. I recommend you do the same for at least the first few years of self-employment.

  Yes, excellent tax preparation software is available that will help you do a good job on your taxes. I've used it for the past ten years after switching to it from the tax pro who formerly did my taxes. But I still recommend that for the first year or two of self-employment you consider working with a professional rather than with a computer program. The tax software has a definite learning curve, and that curve will be less steep if you have as a guide your previous year's tax return that was prepared by a tax professional. Also, meeting with a tax professional as soon as you set up your business will help you get informed about allowable deductions and other things you should be tracking throughout the year. Learn as much as you can from this person before tackling the software on your own.

When you do work with a professional, make sure to get a copy of your tax return for your records. I took this as a given, but it turns out that according to tax preparers, some people do not do this. This indicates to me that they don't realize the value of being able to compare this year's return to last year's return. It also indicates they are being far too trusting and perhaps not thoroughly reviewing the tax return before signing it. When I used a tax professional, I found errors more than once that I needed to point out and have fixed before filing the return. So make sure you not only thoroughly review and understand every line of your return, but that you also get a copy from your tax pro so that you can have it on file. Think of it as a report card on how well your business is doing; by having copies to compare year to year, you can spot places where you can do a better job in the coming year.

- **Take record keeping seriously.** Do *not* be that person who throws receipts and paid invoices into a shoebox and then tries to make sense of it all on April 14. Now that you're making estimated quarterly tax payments, you need to keep on top of your bookkeeping so that you have a solid idea of what those payments should be. The last thing you want to do is guess what these payments should be. If you send in too little money, it can lead to a penalty from the IRS. On the other hand, if you send in too much money, you're in effect lending the IRS your hard-earned cash (and interest free, to boot). Nobody wants to do that.

  Also, you need to track expenses closely to make sure you get all the deductions you deserve. If you're not used to saving receipts, this may be a challenge at first, but it will soon become second nature.

  Develop a method of tracking income and expenses that works for you. Whether you decide to do this on paper or with an accounting software program, keeping this information up-to-date will help you determine your estimated quarterly tax payments with reasonable accuracy. The small business development center at your nearby community college almost certainly offers courses or workshops in QuickBooks accounting software.

  I realize that financial record keeping is an anathema to some people. As a "words person," I'm certainly not fond of typing numbers into a computer program, which is why I am so grateful that my husband does my bookkeeping for me! Perhaps you can work out a similar arrangement with your spouse or significant other. If you don't have such help available, then grit your teeth and just do it . . . or, if your budget allows, pay a bookkeeper.

  Not keeping on top of your numbers not only risks encountering extreme stress when you finally do have to buckle down to the task of doing your taxes, but also means, as I've said, you could be in trouble with the IRS if you have just guesstimated your quarterly tax payments wrong and have underpaid. IRS penalties add up fast, and they are relentless about collecting.

- **Don't get carried away with deductions.** The IRS requires that business deductions be "ordinary and necessary" for the conduct of your business. "Ordinary" means an expense is common and accepted in your field of business. "Necessary" means an expense is helpful and appropriate for your business. Expenses also have to be "reasonable," meaning it is unwise to spend lavishly on anything just because you think it can be deducted. The IRS has guidelines for how much would be a "reasonable" amount for someone in your line of work and earning your income to deduct for specific expense categories. You can get in big trouble—as in called in for an audit—by straying beyond the ordinary, necessary, and reasonable.

  It may be tempting when you first start out to buy the deluxe model of everything on the grounds that it will be deductible. But this can also wreak havoc with your cash flow when the bills flow in for those deluxe models. Playing off current outlays against tax deductions that will come at months down the road isn't always a good strategy.

- **Do learn tax-saving strategies.** You can find plenty of advice on tax-saving strategies online. Just make sure you rely on accredited sources; the IRS website is full of great information, whereas some guy you never heard of who writes a blog may or may not know what he's talking about.

  One tax-saving strategy that has always served me well is to take an inventory of all my office supplies in early December and then head off to the office supply store to buy what I am going to need in the next six months before the end of the month. This way I can deduct this expense on my tax return for the year just ending. I also have planned big purchases, like new computers or laptops, for late in the year to enable me to get the benefit of the deduction sooner rather than later.

  Another key tax-saving area to get up to speed on is retirement plans, as discussed in the previous chapter. Whatever retirement plans you put in place, do develop the discipline to contribute to them monthly rather than waiting until the deadline to dump in your cash. Not only is this a wise strategy for retirement savings, but it is also a wise investing strategy to spread your investments out over the course of the year rather than in one lump sum. (This is called "dollar cost averaging" and means you end up paying less per share over the course of a year than if you made an investment all at once.)

## ✒ Other Voices ✒

**Stefan Lindegaard:** Not staying on top of bookkeeping and tax matters can be a real danger for many—including myself. This is just boring and not productive at all. I am always way behind with my accounting and tax overviews. It works out in the end, but maybe it would be better to pay your way out of this by hiring professional help in order to eliminate such a stress factor.

**Carol Savage:** I have never had difficulty with estimated tax payments. I do let our accountant review my business worksheet and make a recommendation for what I should pay in quarterly payments. Yes, it costs a small sum, but for the most part, it has worked out, and I rarely had to pay in more.

**Barbara Rodriguez:** Ah, yes, the tax man, the bane of my existence. The only thing worse than a bad accountant is a bad lawyer. A tax error can be fixed whereas a legal error can be fatal. During the course of my business, I have had four accountants. I used to think an accountant is an accountant is an accountant. A good accountant can make you or break you. At the beginning when you're making little to no money, it's easy to dismiss the importance of an accountant. Later, as revenues start to increase and you seem to be making less and less because your accountant isn't monitoring your quarterly earnings, you either change accountants or end up paying a big chunk of money at the end of the year, which you may not have readily available. I love my current accountant. He has found ways to save me lots of money, decreased my tax burden, advised me on putting money into a 401K to lessen the tax bite, and changed the structure of my business when necessary. For example, at the beginning I was a sole proprietor, then I became a limited liability corporation, and now an S-Corp. All these structures have tax advantages or disadvantages depending on your particular situation. Find an accountant you can trust, and life will be easier.

**Howie Green:** Don't even try to deal with this stuff on your own. Again, get a good accountant, talk to them every day, and never let him or her go. After my dear, dear lovely, wonderful accountant retired, I found another good one . . . my cousin in San Diego. Location doesn't matter.

# CHAPTER TWENTY

# Deadbeat Clients

Having to chase clients for money is no fun. In fact, it's probably the least fun thing you'll ever do when you're self-employed. It can be an enervating, depressing, and maddening exercise. And it can be downright scary if the amount of money someone owes you is significant enough to put your business in peril.

On this front, I have been amazingly lucky in my years of self-employment because my total financial loss from clients who ultimately never paid for services rendered is under $2,000. (Knock on wood that this continues!) But that doesn't mean I haven't spent nights awake worrying about how much longer I would have to fret about whether this or that client would, in the end, pay what was owed.

I spent months dunning a client in 2009. Promise after promise was broken. I wasn't asking them to pay the few thousand dollars they owed all at once since I knew the recession had knocked their real-estate-related business for a loop. But I did expect them to live up to their promise of paying a small installment each month. But even this proved to be too much for them.

Finally, they had a sudden influx of cash and paid the entire remaining amount off in one fell swoop. Our next conversation dealt with the fact that they were going to have to find a new public relations consultant since I was unwilling to work with them again unless they paid 100 percent in advance. They took it well and, in fact, did pay in full in advance for a project soon after. Lesson learned all the way around.

## The Squeaky Wheel Does Get Oiled

I credit my relatively low losses over nearly three decades of business to the fact that I apply the squeaky wheel adage early and often when a client's bill goes overdue. My bills are supposed to be paid within thirty days; if I don't have a check in hand by day thirty, I e-mail the client on day thirty-one. If that doesn't produce an instant explanation, I follow up with a phone call.

I do not give up, and I don't hesitate to be that irritatingly squeaky wheel. A slow-paying client is guaranteed to hear from me every week. I've found that such persistence is what is required to get invoices paid.

I have friends who will let weeks (or even months!) go by before they inquire about an overdue invoice. This is foolish. As the time expands between when you delivered your services and when you speak up and demand what you are owed, the odds increase that you won't get paid. Einstein didn't come up with that formula, but I am positive it is true based on having observed the losses suffered by colleagues who were loath to do their collections work in a timely fashion.

So, bottom line, if you're the type of person who has a hard time asking for what you deserve (i.e., prompt payment for your product or services), then you may have a rocky road if you go the self-employment route. If this is you, a course in assertiveness may be in order because I guarantee you that sooner or later you will have to chase a client for money. It happens to everyone.

## Coping Strategies

- **Become friends with the person who actually cuts the checks.** I've wrested many a payment out of a late payer by building a good relationship with their accounts payable person. I try to identify this person even before things go haywire so that I don't have to build this relationship *after* a bill is late. Consider calling this person after you submit your first invoice; you can inquire as to whether there was any additional information they needed on the invoice. This positions you as someone who wants to be helpful to them, which they will appreciate.

  Getting on a first-name basis with the accounts payable person will pay dividends down the line; this individual can either make your life miserable or make it a breeze. Never forget this. Also, never get pushy with this person or, worse yet, yell at them. It's not their fault that your client is running short on funds, and a spoonful of sugar will get you much farther than a loud voice will. If the company is in financial troubles or having a cash shortage, the accounts payable person will probably have lots of people being nasty to them. Don't be that person; instead, be the person who is nice and understanding . . . but also persistent.

- **Do not be afraid to play the "I'm not the phone company" card.** I have never hesitated to remind an accounts payable person that I am a solopreneur trying to survive out here on my own instead of a huge faceless corporation with lots of financial resources. Usually you don't have to say too much in this vein to get the message across and have your invoice moved to the top of the pile. Seriously . . . it works, especially if you've laid the groundwork by building a relationship with the accounts payable person.

- **Keep close track of your invoice due dates.** The money end of business is often the least attractive part for many people, especially those of us in creative fields. We hate doing billing, we hate record keeping, and we hate chasing money. Fine. Hate it all you like, but do it anyway if you want to stay in business. You should always know who owes you money, how much they owe, and when it is due.

  Find resources that will help you be well organized and systematic; there are plenty of tools available to assist you in this. For example, a few years ago I started using PayPal to send invoices to my smaller clients, a handful of people for whom I do small editing jobs. Yes, PayPal does take a small cut of the money, but what I've found is that I get my money really fast by using their service because these clients find it quick and easy to pay their small bills (usually no more than a few hundred dollars) through PayPal. My record time between sending out such an invoice and receiving payment was about fifteen minutes!

  Before I started using PayPal for these clients, I often had to waste time chasing down the money. These people are mostly also self-employed people whose systems weren't the best, and so my invoice would shuffle around on their desks, not being paid. That is not the case now, and if someone is a little late, PayPal has a very convenient system that takes just a click of the mouse to send off a friendly reminder.

- **Send invoices electronically.** I hesitated doing this at first, fearing it might not seem professional as an invoice printed on my nice letterhead. But once I did begin to send my invoices via e-mail, I found that they got paid faster. You may find that a small minority of clients will still want you to send them a paper copy of your invoice. For such people, I send both electronically and via snail mail, noting on the electronic invoice that a hard copy is being mailed.

- **See if offering a discount for early payment makes a difference with slow payers.** I've never done this myself, but I do know that small businesses have found it worth their while to offer a small discount of up to 3 percent for early payment. Consider trying this particularly with large invoices that will decimate your available cash if they aren't paid promptly.
- **Ask for deposits.** I have long had a policy that each new client has to pay a deposit until I have enough experience with them to know that they are going to pay their bills promptly. Since I get a huge percentage of my new clients as referrals from existing or former clients, I have always felt a certain amount of protection built in because people usually aren't going to refer someone they know to be a deadbeat. However, no matter how good the source of the referral is, I still always ask for a deposit, usually 20–30 percent. This way, if the new client turns out to have a challenge in paying on time, at least you've got some money up front.
- **Don't be afraid to fire a habitually late-paying client.** I know this is easier said than done, especially if you're just getting started and are trying to build your business. But trust me and all my friends and colleagues who have gone through something like this; firing a lousy client almost always pays off . . . and a client who you have to chase for money is definitely a lousy client. It's the old "when one door closes, another door opens" thing. More often than not, the time you save and the negative energy you avoid by not having to dun someone constantly will mean you have more time to find a good client to replace the bad one. Don't work for people who disrespect you by not paying their bills on time.

    This is not to say that a good client might not need some leeway once or twice. If the person has a reasonable explanation for being late and it has not happened before, of course you cut them some slack. But if this goes on month after month, that's a serious red flag that perhaps this person's business is in trouble and you might be the one holding the (empty) bag in the end.
- **Help avoid collection problems in the first place by researching potential new clients.** As I've mentioned, one of the reasons I think I've been burned so few times with clients who have not paid is that probably 80 percent of my business has come through referrals from either existing clients or close colleagues. In general, you can be fairly certain that these people aren't going to refer anyone about whom they have doubts regarding their ability to pay. But for those potential clients

who come your way from other sources (your website, through meeting them at a networking meeting, and the like), you should definitely do as much research as you can before signing on with them.

For example, check the Better Business Bureau website to see if they have complaints about them. If a business is shoddy in one aspect of their work, such as customer service, you can bet that they might be sloppy in another aspect, such as paying their vendors. Also, check with people in your business network to see if anyone knows anything about how the business treats its vendors. If anything sounds questionable, back away. It's easier and better to find another prospect than it is to tie yourself to a company that is going to make you beg for the money you are owed.

## ✎ Other Voices ✎

**Stefan Lindegaard:** I have not really experienced bad clients who did not pay their bills, but I have had my share of clients who took a very long time to pay. I have learned that even though big companies start out with a sixty- to ninety-days payment term, you can bring this down to something more acceptable. Not everything is written in stone, not even at these big companies. State your case and ask for fairness. It sometimes helps.

**Barbara Rodriguez:** I've never really had to worry about deadbeat clients since most of my clients are government agencies. We also work with large hospitals, health clinics, and the like. More small businesses should consider working with the government. The government buys just about any product or service. Don't let the RFPs or the bureaucratic red tape scare you. Once you establish yourself, there's a lot of money to be made, and they don't become deadbeat because you have an official contract with them spelling out the payment terms. Once you get a contract with one state, it's easy to piggyback on that to procure a contract in another state. You need to show some track record. You also need to know the exact person to call if payment on invoices start lagging. Many people are scared to work with the government, but I find them to be very reliable customers as long as you cross your *i*'s and dot your *t*'s and stay competitive. State contracts offer stability and security because they usually go for a certain term, like three to five years. The state can only work with vendors who have been approved, and, if applicable, you can get certified as a minority- or woman-owned business, which is beneficial since the state has to dedicate a percentage of their contracting out to minority- or woman-owned businesses.

**Howie Green:** I always worked with a collection agency, and if clients don't pay their bills, then I don't work for them anymore. Simple as that. They wouldn't accept nonpayment from their clients, and why should I? This is business, so you have to make sure both you and your client have the same payment expectations and keep to those expectations. Thirty days, forty-five days, sixty days—whatever the payment schedule is, make sure everyone is clear about it. And the best advice I ever got was from my accountant, who said, "If your clients aren't complaining about how much you charge, then you're not charging enough!"

# CHAPTER TWENTY-ONE

# Surviving Cash Flow Ebbs

Earlier, I talked about the problem of having big fluctuations in your work-load. An obvious corollary of a downswing in your workload is an ensuing drop in your income. Developing strategies for surviving cash flow ebbs means the difference between staying in business for yourself and needing to hunt for a gig with a regular paycheck.

In real estate, everyone knows the most important thing is "location, location, location." It didn't take me long to realize when I started my business that "cash flow, cash flow, cash flow" rules the life of the self-employed. Having a steady, adequate influx of money to pay the bills is essential. This is especially true if you're single, and there is no one else around to serve as your financial backstop if your income suddenly takes a dive.

Aside from the practical worries of having bills that need to be paid, a slowdown in your income may affect your mental capacity to focus on your work, causing your self-confidence and optimism about your future to plum-met. This is especially true if you're in the early days of self-employment and haven't been down this road before. It is easy to panic and be filled with self-doubt about the career choice you've made.

## Avoid Feeling Nostalgic

You may find yourself nostalgic for that former job and its reliable paycheck. You might polish up your résumé and spend time perusing online job sites. This is not the route out, however. Do not beat yourself up over the choice you've made to try self-employment and do not lose faith in your ability to make it on your own. Instead, stay focused on the two tasks at hand: 1) providing excellent service for your clients and 2) undertaking activities that will bring in new business. In my experience, if you're doing these two things, something will turn up to turn your finances around.

I know that following this advice takes an act of faith, but I urge you to stick with it. Once you've been through a couple slowdowns in your cash flow, you'll gain confidence in your ability to turn things around. I barely blinked when I lost my biggest client when the Great Recession hit in late 2007 because I had been there/done that in the two previous recessions I'd survived. After nearly two decades of self-employment, I was confident I could go out and find someone else who needed my services. As it turned out, only a month later, I didn't find a new client—he found me all the way from the other side of the Atlantic Ocean via my website! And he's still my client all these years later.

Learning to manage your cash flow is an essential skill. As I've mentioned before, the wise thing is to create a rainy-day fund, setting aside money when your business is really rocking to help during the inevitable lulls. Despite being a total bust at assembling a rainy-day fund, I have managed to master the cash flow management strategies below, which have kept me out of trouble and will help you too.

## Coping Strategies

- **Get deposits.** Getting part of your money up front is always a wise idea and definitely helps with cash flow crunches. I only require new clients to pay deposits, but the fact is that the time when you're out beating the new businesses' bushes the hardest is during cash flow lulls, so it's also when you're likely to have new clients from which to request deposits.

  Don't hesitate to use this strategy. It is common business practice, and if a would-be client balks at it, it is a signal that perhaps you'll have a hard time getting your money once you have done the work.

  I also know people who require deposits from ongoing clients. In general, however, I think it's difficult to switch strategies once a relationship has already begun. If you suddenly start asking for deposits on every project, this may give the impression you're in financial trouble. In general, people don't like doing business with vendors who are on the financial ropes because they wonder if you'll be around long enough to finish the job. I make one exception to this: If you've learned from painful experience that a client tends to be a slow payer, by all means start asking for deposits. Instead of being left waiting for all of your money at the end of a project, at least you'll already have collected part of it.

- **Have retainer clients.** This doesn't work in every business, but if you're a consultant like me, it definitely helps to have some clients on retainer. Terms can vary, but in most cases, it means you get paid at the start of the month for work that will be done in that month. This gives you predictability in your income, at least as long as the retainer agreement continues. In exchange for paying up front each month, I give clients a small discount on my hourly rate (usually 10 percent). But again, not everybody does it; some people charge their normal rate for retainers.

- **Don't be afraid to be a nag.** Sometimes cash flow problems are caused not by a slow work period but by a client who is slow to pay. As I discussed in the last chapter, being diligent about reminding clients when bills are overdue is essential.

  Many times, I've had friends complain that one of their clients hasn't paid . . . sometimes for months! When I ask what they've done about it, the answer has sometimes been "Nothing." Too many freelancers are so afraid of ruffling a client's feathers that they hesitate to implement good collection practices. This is madness. You did the work; you deserve to be paid and paid on time. If you don't have the backbone to ask for the money you are owed, self-employment almost certainly is not for you.

- **Don't hesitate to drop a client who is constantly late with payments.** Almost any client can sometimes lose your bill in the clutter on their desk or go off on vacation without remembering that your payment is due. But if a client is consistently late paying and you have to constantly nag to get what is due you, this probably signals that the client is in financial trouble and may be on their way out of business. You don't want to be among the unpaid creditors when they shut their doors. So bid them a gracious good-bye and find a client without such problems. (It should go without saying that you wait to say adieu until after you've collected what is currently due . . . and *never* keep doing additional work for someone who is seriously overdue on their payment to you.)

  I also believe that having to deal with the negativity of repeatedly having to dun a client is something you're better off without. It is energy sapping to have to gear yourself up for yet another phone conversation in which you ask to be paid, only to be given more excuses and promises that more than likely are quickly broken. You'll feel so much better when you've put such a client in your rearview mirror that you'll have plenty of positive energy to go out and find a client to replace the late-payer.

- **Do without the convenience of automatic bill payments.** Sure, having your mortgage, credit card, utility bills, and other payments automatically deducted from your checking account each month is hugely convenient. But when you're self-employed and experience a cash flow crisis, those automatic payments can lead to disaster. You need to be aware of your bank balance at all times and be able to decide whom to pay when based on your estimates of when clients will pay what they owe you. Doing without the automatic payments is a pain, I know, but you need to retain as much financial flexibility as possible.

- **Don't keep it a secret if you need more business.** The tendency among many self-employed people who hit a financial slump is to hide this development from colleagues who are in a position to help. The desire to have people think you're highly successful is natural, and certainly you don't want to go around with a gloomy face complaining about how poor you are. However, a middle ground exists between giving the impression that you are doing so well that you couldn't possibly take on a new client and having people worry that you might go out of business any day now.

  Don't let your ego keep you from reaching out to friends. There is no shame in letting a select group of people know that you could use more business. I've often found that a quiet word to one of my close collaborators that my schedule isn't as full as I'd like it to be has produced a timely referral or a subcontracting opportunity that makes all the difference. I have also been prompted to similarly send business toward colleagues when they have shared with me that their business was in a bit of a slow spot.

---

### ✐ Other Voices ✐

**Stefan Lindegaard:** I know all about cash flow ebbs, but somehow it seems as if it just works out. You might be a bit late on some payments, but you get through it . . . once again. You kind of get a strong stomach when you have been through this over and over again. I think most other people with regular jobs would be running away like crazy if they did not know if they could pay the bills two months ahead. Of course, this also means that one of the things I really strive for as a lifestyle entrepreneur is to get to the point where I don't have to worry about this. You get used to it, but the cash flow ebbs can still bring you down.

**Barbara Rodriguez:** At the beginning, I would deposit payments once a week. I soon learned that if I deposited payments as they came in—sometimes daily—my cash flow improved and I felt much better psychologically. After we could show some track record of success, I applied for a line of credit. I have never had to use it, but it gave me a sense of security.

Early on, I also felt shy about collections. I soon—out of necessity—overcame my shyness and found that most of the time, the invoice has been sitting forgotten on someone's desk and they apologize profusely and send the payment. So I started staying right on top of due dates and being proactive about collections. I also now call the accounts payable departments to request EFT payments if possible. This lowers the possibility that the invoice will fall into a black hole on someone's desk. The invoice should go to the right person to begin with, or maybe consider cc'ing the accounts payable person.

**Howie Green:** I had a great accountant who, as part of his very reasonably priced service, monitored my account and told me when to pay bills and what bills to pay. If it were up to me, it would have been a mess. GET A GOOD ACCOUNTANT!

# CHAPTER TWENTY-TWO

# Six Things That Make Self-Employment Worthwhile

Need a break from pondering the financial challenges of being self-employed? Let's shake off those worries by looking at the upside of being your own boss. After all, I don't want to discourage you from trying to go it alone. And obviously, I must have good things to say about being your own boss or else I surely wouldn't have been out here on my own for nearly thirty years now!

Here are the top six things I enjoy about being self-employed.

### 1) Choosing Which Clients I Want to Work with and Those to Whom I Say, "No, Thanks."

As I've mentioned, my last days as someone else's employee were spent working for a Boston public relations firm. There I sometimes found myself sitting across a conference room table from a client I didn't much like. This in part happened because most of that firm's business was with real estate developers. Some of them were great—even inspiring—people. But in the late 1980s, that industry also seemed to attract a disproportionate share of egomaniacs with grandiose ideas about how important and newsworthy their current projects were. Or at least that was the case during the real estate boom that Boston was then experiencing, when quick-buck artists were plentiful. Also, I've never met anyone who would haggle more over price than a real estate developer. They wanted maximum results for a minimum dent in their budget.

One night, I found myself driving home around eleven o'clock from a town meeting in Belmont, Massachusetts, where our clients were trying to get approval for a small project. It was snowing like crazy on Route 128, and all I could think of in the near whiteout conditions was that I was going to drive off the road, go down an embankment, and not be found for hours. The fact that the developers in question were not very nice people hardly made me feel better about my impending demise. These were not people I would have chosen to work with if I'd had an option. (And yes, I do realize this is easy for me to say; I wasn't the one who had to sign the payroll checks every other week, so I can't really criticize the agency owner for agreeing to work with some developers who had money but no manners.)

But since becoming my own boss, I have had the option of saying yes or no to a prospective client. When I turn down business because I don't think the personality fit is right between the prospective client and me, the sense of freedom is great. It's so much easier and more motivating to work with clients you really like than with clients you'd prefer not to be around. So I ask myself, "Would I like to hang out with this person?" If the answer is "No, I wouldn't particularly care to have lunch with him/her," then I usually take a pass on the business.

## 2) The Freedom to Work at Home, Set My Own Hours, and Organize My Life the Way I Want It Organized

I am a night person by nature, so having the choice to *not* get out of bed at the crack of dawn, get gussied up, and commute to work suits me just fine. If I feel like sleeping in, I do. Sure, I may work longer in the afternoon or evening to make up for that extra hour of sleep in the morning, but for a night owl like me, it's worth it. And if I decide to take Fridays off in the summer, nobody is going to say, "No, you can't do that." The same is true for picking my vacation weeks.

This control over my time also means I can go to the gym or go grocery shopping in the middle of the afternoon when these places are much less busy than they are if you have to go after work or on the weekends. I also can take time off during the day for volunteer work, or, if the writing muse just isn't with me on a given day, I can grab a book to read, go for a walk, or do anything else that strikes my fancy.

Also, I spend my summer days barefoot and wearing shorts and a T-shirt and my winter days in jeans and a fleece top. Once in a while, I do have to go meet with a client, but not nearly as often as I did back when I first started freelancing. People nowadays seem quite happy to work via phone and e-mail. I even have several clients in faraway locations who I've never met, including one in Denmark with whom I have written several books. Technology is grand, isn't it?

### 3) Ability to Control My Own Fate

This is perhaps the biggest benefit of being self-employed. When you are working for someone else, they ultimately decide what direction your career is going to take, how far and how fast you are going to rise up the career ladder, or whether you'll get kicked to the curb.

For the first ten years or so after I left corporate life, I wondered if I'd made a serious mistake. I was living in Boston at the time and had plenty of friends who worked at big companies where I knew they had nice benefit packages. I once had those same kinds of packages—great health insurance for next to no money, a good pension, four weeks of paid vacation, profit sharing—the works. Then bad things began to happen to my friends. As I mentioned earlier, when Polaroid was driven into the ground by bad management in 2001, I had friends who lost all the money they'd invested in Polaroid stock through the employee stock ownership plan. Not long after, the life insurance company where I had worked for eight years was bought out by an industry giant, and jobs were lost left and right. At the time, I thought about how that could have been my fate if I'd stayed on there.

And this continued into the Great Recession. I got a phone call from a former colleague and longtime friend who had worked at Fidelity Investments for well over a decade. She had lost her job and was starting her freelance writing business up again . . . in the middle of one of the worst economic downturns ever. I felt very badly for her at the time, although I'm happy to report she managed to make a go of it.

Because of events like these, I stopped envying my friends in corporate life long ago. Yes, it has been challenging to be self-employed through three recessions. And, sure, I sometimes wish someone other than me was paying for my health insurance or that I didn't have to pay the whole Social Security tax without help from an employer. But the joy in knowing that my fate is in my own hands and not in someone else's is worth all of that and more.

### 4) Having Control over the Direction Your Business Takes

Back in 1999, after I'd been self-employed for a decade, I felt the need for a new, more intellectual challenge. So I decided I wanted to ghostwrite books. This involved taking a significant risk of devoting hours and hours of nonpaid time to write a book proposal and sample chapters with one of my clients. Then we had to find an agent and a publisher, neither of which is easy. But getting that first book published enabled me to begin pulling in more book ghostwriting assignments, a field I still work in today.

If you're working for someone else, your ability to change up your career direction like this is limited. In most companies, you have to fit yourself into the job your employer wants you to do rather than being able to choose the direction in which you want to take the job. You can, of course, opt to find another employer, but this can be easier said than done, especially if the direction you wish to take your career is significantly different from your prior experience. If, on the other hand, you're self-employed, you are the master of what you will do as long as you can find a market for it.

## 5) Being the Decision Maker

Just as you can choose to take your business in any direction you want to, you also are in charge of every other decision regarding the business and how it operates. Not that you will necessarily always get every decision right. I know I've made mistakes along the way; everyone does. But at least you won't be at the whim of someone else's bad judgment, and you won't have a micromanager looking over your shoulder and second-guessing everything you do. I can't tell you how liberating this feels when you fully realize that you don't have to answer to anyone.

Of course, there are people who prefer to have someone else make the decisions and people for whom making big decisions is agonizing. If this sounds like you, then self-employment probably is not your game.

## 6) Ability to Relocate If You Want To

I've moved my business twice in the past twelve years. I moved from one end of Massachusetts to the other in 2002. Then, in August 2013, I moved to North Carolina, where the cheaper cost of living will enable me to fully retire in a few years. Thanks to the wonders of the Internet and because of the nature of my business, neither of these moves materially affected my ability to keep the business thriving. When I moved from Boston to western Massachusetts, I kept my Boston clients. Of course, I was only ninety minutes out the Mass. Pike, so that wasn't much of a change, really. But when I moved to North Carolina, I kept my Massachusetts clients . . . and my client in Denmark and my client in Texas and my client in Rhode Island—well, you get the idea.

I have a number of self-employed friends who have made similar moves. One of my western Massachusetts friends moved her web design business to Nashville a couple years ago and continued to work with her Bay State clients from there. One friend, a headhunter who finds executives for insurance companies, now spends half his year in Florida and the other half in New England. Try doing that when you're part of Corporate America!

Of course, not all fields lend themselves to this type of mobility, but plenty do. And while some companies do allow employees to work from remote locations, this is not yet an option that is available to everyone. So if you want to have the ability to relocate at some point, self-employment will give you the ability to do that in many cases.

## ✐ Other Voices ✐

**Stefan Lindegaard:** Another good thing about self-employment is that you get to meet many like-minded people. It just gives you extra energy when others around you are passionate about their jobs and businesses.

**Barbara Rodriguez:** I planned my business so I could work remotely. We never see customers in person. Our customers schedule interpreters by phone, fax, or e-mail, and our translation customers send documents by e-mail, which we work on and return by e-mail. It's all electronically driven, and with technology today, just about anything can be accomplished electronically. This is one of the features I like best about my business. We can work from anywhere, even Aruba!

**Howie Green:** For me, one of the best things about being self-employed is being able to work with a variety of clients and do a variety of projects at the same time. On any given day, I am doing an illustration or designing a poster or a logo or a publication or a PowerPoint presentation. It keeps the creative juices flowing.

Also, with my smart phone and iPad, I can do my business from anywhere. I stopped telling my clients when I'm traveling years ago because I realized it makes no difference anymore.

**Pat Mullaly:** I love taking vacations! And as a freelance designer, I have managed to integrate work with travel without any problems.

When the weather grows too cold for comfort here in the Northeast, I've rented a condo in Florida for a month or two and worked from there. I usually let my clients know as physical proofs of print jobs need to be delivered and approved between us, but other than that, there's no reason not to just take off and go when my spirit decides to explore.

PART IV

# POTENTIAL ROADBLOCKS
# TO SUCCESS

# CHAPTER TWENTY-THREE

# The Double
# Whammy of Health Issues

Twice in 2013, I was reminded yet again of one of the biggest perils of self-employment. In July, my right retina detached again—for the third time. Following surgery in July, which involved putting a gas bubble in my eye, I was ordered to stay in bed on my left side for a week . . . not something anyone who is self-employed wants to hear. Also, the gas used for the air bubble this time around would take over three months to dissolve, so I was working with one eye throughout that period. (This time period also coincided with my move from western Massachusetts to Durham, North Carolina. If you want to have a nightmare road trip, try driving nearly seven hundred miles with one eye . . . and a semisedated yet still screaming cat in a cage on the back seat!)

For three months, I waited for the gas bubble to dissipate, assuming I would regain my full vision, as had occurred the two previous times I had had this procedure done. But the vision turned out to be blurry, so it was back into the operating room again in November—this time with a new surgeon in North Carolina.

Fortunately, this time, the post-op routine was not a disaster; my new doctor said I only had to take it easy for twenty-four hours before I was able to be up and at my desk again. But it was another three months of wearing an eye patch waiting for the air bubble to go away. This time around, my vision ended up being slightly better, although still not perfect when it comes to reading, a definite handicap for someone in my line of work.

## A Financial Double Whammy

Each of these incidences, of course, also involved unexpected medical expenses. Since I have Medicare coverage now, the damage to my wallet for these last two surgeries only totaled $500, much less than the $2,000 deductible I had paid three or four years previously for this same surgery *before* I qualified for Medicare and had what was pretty lousy, albeit expensive, health insurance.

Anyone who is self-employed lives in fear of such health scares because they can potentially be a double whammy to your finances; they can cost you money on medical bills while simultaneously interfering with your ability to earn money and keep the cash flowing. And, if you are also single, there is no Plan B . . . no backup plan in which a partner or spouse can help tide you over if you hit a financial rough spot due to illness.

Such events are something anyone who is considering self-employment needs to seriously consider. Cash flow is king when you're self-employed. If you have a medical condition that might periodically jeopardize your cash flow, you definitely need to squirrel away a good-sized emergency fund to tide you over any such potential bumps in the road. And having disability income insurance, although expensive, might be wise.

## Disobeying Doctor's Orders

To be honest, I am giving you advice here that I have never managed to follow myself, although I did have disability income insurance for about twelve years. I didn't run into my first medical problem until I was three years into self-employment, when I suffered a torn retina in my left eye. This was my first experience with such surgery, and the damage was severe enough that it required a four-day hospital stay instead of the in-and-out-the-same-day surgeries that I've subsequently had when the retina in my right eye tore.

With this first surgery, the surgeon advised that I should take it easy and not plan to work for a month to six weeks. This presented two big problems. First, I was in the middle of organizing a major community event for one of my biggest clients. I did have a subcontractor who was helping me with the work, but I was the one doing all the interacting with the client and with the public schools and the local newspaper that were involved in the program.

Second, I had no emergency fund to tide me over. I had started my business a few years earlier just as the economy entered a significant recession from which we were just recovering. Those first years I hung on by my fingertips in terms of finances, and I was finally beginning to see light at the end of a long tunnel, but I had not yet been able to build up significant savings. So, as far as I was concerned, not earning any income for a month or more wasn't an option.

The afternoon I returned home from the hospital, I was on the phone assuring the client that all was well and that there would be no interruption in the planning of their event. I took things fairly easy for a few days, but by the next week, I was working a normal schedule.

The only thing I didn't do until the patch came off my eye six weeks later was drive to client meetings. While it is legal to drive with vision in only one eye, trying this feat on the busy highways around Greater Boston—where drivers wear their aggressiveness like a badge of honor—was not something I was eager to try. Friends were kind enough to pitch in and take me the few places I had to go. For example, one couple in my condo complex took me with them when they did their weekly grocery shopping. Another friend drove me to my eye doctor for the checkups I needed.

I was lucky in that the type of work I do rarely involves anything truly strenuous. Once I got a few nights of good rest after the hospitalization, my energy level was back to normal. I could easily manage sitting at my desk all day writing and making phone calls. The doctor did impose a few rules about physical movement (no lifting anything over five pounds, for example), but they posed no problem. The only real physical challenge I faced was that my good eye got really tired if I stayed at my computer too long. I tried to manage this by taking frequent breaks during the day.

## Stressed Much?

Was this a stressful period? You bet! The possibility of going blind in one eye was a real threat when the retina first tore. The risk of having a significant gap in my income was very real too. It didn't materialize, though, but only because I ignored the doctor's advice to not work for a month. But, of course, with many medical problems, it is not feasible to ignore an order not to work. For example, I was so weakened by abdominal surgery I had years before I became self-employed that I could not return to work for a full six weeks. Thank heaven that the checks kept flowing from my employer! If such an event had occurred once I was self-employed, I have no idea what I would have done.

What will you do if your health lets you down while you're self-employed? What if your ability to work for a lengthy period of time is threatened? Obviously, if your line of work requires physical labor or frequent travel, you could be limited in your ability to continue working if any significant medical woes arise.

Do you have enough savings or another source of income such as an employed spouse or partner to help you make it through a period of inactivity? These are things to think through in advance, and particularly so if you have any type of recurring medical condition. And even if you have no health challenges, it is wise to remember we're all one slip on an icy sidewalk away from potential disaster.

## Coping Strategies

- **Be aware of your risk tolerance.** Financial planners often advise people to consider their risk tolerance when choosing investments. You should do the same by considering whether you could tolerate being in a situation where a medical emergency might jeopardize your income. If you are someone whose tolerance for financial risk is low, self-employment may not be your best bet.

  I've never missed a payment on any of my bills, but there have been times when things were cut very close, usually when a big client failed to pay on time. If living with such possibilities makes you nervous just thinking about it, you might be better off not sticking your financial neck out. Or at the very least, be sure you follow the advice below about amassing an emergency fund that would relieve your stress if a medical crisis does occur.

- **Buy the best health insurance you can afford.** Health insurance has often been a major sticking point with people who have wanted to join the ranks of the self-employed but felt they couldn't leave their employer-provided health insurance for any number of reasons. Options for self-employed people greatly improved with the advent of the Affordable Care Act, both in terms of affordability and the breadth of coverage available.

  Over the years, I've had self-employed friends who went without health insurance, saying they couldn't afford it. Then I'd notice they were planning a European vacation or doing an expensive home renovation. "Ah, that's where their health insurance money is going," I'd think.

  I'm a risk-taker, but this is one risk that is not worth taking. Medical bills are the chief cause of bankruptcy in the United States. Nearly two million people filed bankruptcy in 2013 because of unpaid medical bills, making this the biggest cause of personal bankruptcies.

- **Consider disability income insurance.** But do your homework carefully on this and make sure you go with one of the most credible providers. Too many times, insurers deny claims, contending that the disabilities do not meet the definitions held in their policies. I cancelled my policy after reading media coverage of the disability insurance industry that made it clear that it was unlikely that an insurer would ever agree that I was totally disabled based on the highly sedentary nature of my occupation. As long as I am able to type, see the monitor, and talk on the phone, I can work at my chosen profession. But if your occupation poses much more physical challenges than mine does, this type of insurance, although expensive, is well-worth considering.

- **Amass an emergency fund.** Having six to eight months of income squirreled away will come in handy not only if a medical emergency strikes that prevents you from working but to help you during all sorts of other problematic times as well. Again, I have not practiced what I'm preaching, and as a result, I've faced my share of financial stresses. It has been more due to good luck than good management that I've always managed to stay afloat financially. My ability to tolerate risk has served me well, but not everyone can manage doing a financial high-wire act with no safety net. So do a better job than I have and get your emergency fund in the bank and alleviate yourself of sleepless nights.

## ✐ Other Voices ✐

**Mark G. Auerbach:** I can relate to Jeanne's eye issues. I've had four retinal surgeries in three years. I should have known better about disability insurance. I had a somewhat expensive policy when I started out, but I let it lapse, because I couldn't afford the premiums. Fast-forward twenty-five years. I can't get one now, because I have diabetes, which is considered a "preexisting condition." When you start out in business, insure yourself. You are your business, and if you can't work, no money comes in.

**Barbara Rodriguez:** It's not just *your* health that can let you down. It's also the health of your loved ones and those around you. Back in September of 2006, my partner was diagnosed with cancer. I had just moved into the small business incubator in Springfield, Massachusetts, and the future was looking very positive. My business was really taking off, and I had the incubator committee to work with and to report to quarterly. Everything was on me since I still hadn't hired any additional staff. When I look back on that time, everything is a blur. My partner and I were driving back and forth to Mass General in Boston weekly for chemo treatments. Through it all, I was lucky enough to meet someone who changed the course of my business, who was trustworthy and energetic, and who had the desire for us to succeed— Jessica Ridley. She knew my predicament, and she took the reins. She is now our operations manager, and annual revenues have grown to over $1,000,000. In my case, things turned out positively, but in many cases, it would not have. You must prepare for the unexpected and think about different "what if" scenarios. Now, I have disability and life insurance on my key employees, as well as myself. Like I always say, better to have it and not need it than to need it and not have it.

**Carol Savage:** Like many baby boomers, I had aging parents with many health, financial, and planning needs. My dad was diagnosed with Alzheimer's, and my mother didn't drive. Caring for aging parents is an act of love, but it's also tremendously stressful and definitely impacts your business. Managing their day-to-day needs while trying to keep your clients happy is a tough balancing act. While I'm happy to have had the privilege of caring for my parents, it took a large toll on my business. For two years, I managed to keep my head just above water, and new business and marketing efforts ground to a halt. I don't know what advice to offer except maybe have a colleague in mind to help you if backup is needed. If you can proactively do some of this parent care and financial planning in advance, then do it. Ask others in your family to manage certain aspects of your parents' care, so you don't have to do it alone. It's something I hadn't anticipated, and looking back, I had no idea how time-consuming and stressful it would turn out to be.

# CHAPTER TWENTY-FOUR

# Alliances Gone Wrong

One of the best ways for someone who is self-employed to grow his/her business is to form strategic alliances with people in related fields. For example, graphic designers and web designers have been a great source of new business for me through the years since they frequently have clients who need help with writing brochure copy, website copy, or other materials. In turn, if I come across a client who needs a graphic designer, I refer them to one of my colleagues. At the same time, however, it is important to understand if an alliance goes off the rails, it can pose a considerable danger to your business.

With one notable exception, I've been very lucky with my alliances. But I have witnessed several alliances among self-employed individuals that have gone horribly, horribly wrong. When a blowup of this nature occurs, it often leads to very bad feelings and, in some extreme cases, can even imperil someone's business. The two lessons I have learned from witnessing these events and from one episode of my own where things went terribly awry are:

1. Don't enter into an alliance with someone you don't know *really* well.
2. Be clear what your expectations are, especially when it comes to money and who controls what.

## Working with a Fool

The only bad alliance-related experience I have had in my freelance career also happened to be the situation in which I took my biggest financial bath ever. It taught me a big lesson about making sure I knew who I was, meta-phorically speaking, getting into bed with before agreeing to partner with someone. A print broker I didn't know called me and said several people had recommended me to him as a possible writer for a marketing brochure for one of his clients. I didn't know the guy from Adam, and I should have done more homework and gotten some references on him. But the job was attractive in terms of my fee, so I readily agreed to meet with him and his client and the graphic designer he had brought into the job, who was also someone I didn't know.

It was clear early on that the client required lots of hand-holding because he had never worked with freelancers before. That was fine; I'm used to that. We had several overly long meetings while we all worked to educate him on how this process worked. Things seemed to be going smoothly.

However, once my writing was done and the designer, who turned out to be a real pro, had come up with a design the client liked, I was shocked to hear that we had all been fired! Turns out that weeks earlier while the print broker sat in the client's lobby waiting for a meeting, the client's assistant began complaining to him about how unhappy she was in her job. The print broker generously suggested that she apply for a job at his wife's firm. She had been offered a job at a higher salary, and our client had to give her a raise to keep her!

The client was understandably upset with the idea of a vendor tampering with his staff, and who could blame him? I thought it was one of the dumb-est moves I'd ever heard of and was appalled. Although the client said he knew neither the designer nor I had anything to do with the print broker's gaffe, the whole thing left such a bad taste in his mouth that he refused to pay us the remainder of our fee, which in my case was over $1,000. Since the contract was between the print broker and the client, I had no legal recourse. Lesson learned . . . make sure you're not partnering with an idiot!

## Why Are We Doing This?

I've seen friends make the mistake I made of not getting to know someone well or failing to check references. But in most cases where I've seen friends that have alliances go awry, the cause has been a failure to set expectations up front. This applies to money, responsibilities, and power. (Power in this situation refers to who is in charge and who "owns" the client relationship.)

Have a candid discussion about what you want out of the relationship. When everyone puts their cards on the table up front, things are apt to go much more smoothly over the long haul. For example, I have one web designer colleague who expects me to pay a 10 percent finder's fee when she refers a client to me. Ditto if I refer a client to her. It works well because we decided that in advance of any referrals being made, not after.

Also make sure your personalities are a good match. You don't want to be frequently working with someone you aren't really simpatico with, do you? Dealing with difficult clients is maddening enough, let alone adding a difficult colleague into the mix.

Of course, the degree of care you take in choosing someone to work with will differ based on how long or how close the relationship is expected to be. In my case with the print broker, I saw this as just a one-off deal, and since two people who were part of a networking group I belonged to had given him my name, I didn't think I needed to check him out more carefully. My mistake! But if you're going to enter into a true alliance where you're intending to share clients over the long term and will be doing activities such as joint marketing, you need to do much more homework and much more strategizing together about the objectives and the mechanics of the relationship.

Here's an example of why this is critical. One of my former clients brought a younger woman into her business as a name partner. This younger woman was at a very different stage of life than my client was; she had a young child at home while my clients' children were through college. The new partner wanted a lifestyle business that would leave her plenty of time to not only see to her child's needs but also to pursue other interests, such as remodeling her house.

When it came to activities that weren't generating revenue for her, such as marketing, she gave good lip service but rarely actually followed through. This left the marketing up to my client, which was exactly what she had been trying to avoid when she partnered up with the new person. After over a decade in a solo business, my client was looking forward to having someone else handle part of the marketing load. But alas, it was quickly clear that this wasn't going to happen . . . or if it did, it would only be in fits and starts. (For example, the last time I checked the blog the new partner had begun, she had posted nothing in the last six months. Not exactly impressive in a world in which you're better off not having a blog than having one where it's clear to the world that you quickly ran out of interest in posting.)

## Coping Strategies

- **If you're hoping for a long-term alliance or partnership, learn how the other person conducts business and treats clients.** The tendency when talk turns to forming an alliance is to focus on how well your service offerings match up with those of the other person. But if you don't ensure from the start that you have the same attitude toward how to conduct business and how to treat clients and customers, you're in for a world of trouble.

Before starting to talk about strategies for aligning and who will be responsible for various activities, talk first about your objectives for your businesses. Listen carefully to how the other person talks about their clients. Do they seem to value their clients and enjoy working with them or do they say negative things about them? Do they seem to put the interests of their clients first and to be committed to delivering the best work possible and to meeting deadlines? Or do you get the sense that they try to nickel and dime their clients to death and tend to play loosey-goosey with deadlines? If the business habits and attitudes of a potential alliance partner don't match yours, walk away and do it quickly. If you don't, you're going to face an endless series of arguments and may end up doing serious harm to your business reputation.

- **Find out as much as you can about the clients of your potential partner.** As I mentioned earlier, one of the things I enjoy most about being self-employed is the freedom to choose my own clients. Depending on how close an alliance you form, you may be giving away some of this freedom. If you're going to be working with the existing clients of a new ally (and not just going after new clients together), you want to make sure that you'll be comfortable with these clients.

Over the years, I have delved into referrals I received from an alliance partner only to find out they were in no way the type of person I'd want to work with. One memorable case that caused some bad blood between an ally and me involved a man who wanted help with a book he was writing. When the name was presented to me, I did what I usually do with any referral and Googled the guy. Imagine my surprise when a bunch of stories about the fairly significant white-collar crime he had committed and served time for popped up!

This man's crime was widely covered in the local media, but that was before I moved to the region, so I knew nothing about it. I quickly explained to my colleague that as someone who is in the public relations business, I couldn't work for this client without potentially doing damage to my own reputation. Other clients would not want to be linked with him, even if only on my client list. Nor would they want the media knowing that I worked for them *and* for this former felon. My ally suggested that I do the work and just not tell anyone. Yeah, right. We lived in a very small region where word of almost everything got out sooner or later. I was not going to risk my reputation, and neither did I want to have anything to do with a book of business advice from a guy who had gone to jail for bad business practices!

Anyway, you get my point. If your potential ally has any dubious characters on their client list, you'll want to know about this in advance. You should also agree on whether there are types of clients you will not pursue together. For example, at the PR firm I worked for the management team agreed that we would not work on tobacco accounts.

- **If you're forming a partnership on which you'll be working together in every aspect of the business, make sure you have matching career goals.** I've seen partnerships falter because people have different objectives; one may want a lifestyle business that leaves them plenty of time for other interests, while the person they're aligning with is willing to devote themselves full time to growing a strong business with a constantly growing revenue stream. Trying to make this type of relationship work is nearly impossible.

- **Try baby steps first.** Dipping your toe in the water with a small joint project instead of going headlong into announcing to the world that you're entering a major alliance is often the best way to go. This gives both of you a chance to see how the other works with clients and to judge whether their skill level matches what they claim to have. If problems are uncovered, you can either figure out a way to address those or bow out of the alliance. This will save you the embarrassment of having announced an alliance only to have to acknowledge in short order that it didn't work out.

- **Put key points in writing.** This should not need to be said, but, alas, from my observations of others, it is advice that is frequently ignored, to everyone's later regret. Going through the exercise of putting in writing the key points of an alliance is very helpful. While you may not be forming a legal partnership, you still will benefit from putting down the key points, especially those related to money and responsibilities. And, of course, if you are forming a legal partnership, then make sure you have all your paperwork ducks in order on that front before moving forward.

## ✑ Other Voices ✑

**Stefan Lindegaard:** Some warnings here: Not all alliances pay off. Not all networking efforts or new business contacts are worth pursuing. This kind of stuff takes up lots of time, and too often you realize that you will get nothing out of it.

**Mark G. Auerbach:** I was brought on board a project by another marketing agency, and although the client seemed to like my recommendations, they weren't always implemented because the agency that hired me didn't like them. When the client became aware that certain recommendations weren't implemented, the other agency said I'd not followed through. I had to convince the client that the agency was the one not following up. Ultimately, I was hired by the client and told to supervise the other agency, which resigned the account. Nice guys do finish first, and can be the ones to point out deficiencies in work arrangements that don't best benefit the company.

**Carol Savage:** I have a very serious red flag reaction when it comes to new business. In twenty-four years of freelancing, it has rarely been wrong. If you get a red flag about a potential new client or project, your instincts are telling you to stay away. Nine out of ten times after I've declined a piece of business that induced my red flag, I've invariably heard stories about someone else working with the client and the nightmares that prevailed. So pay attention to your red flag!

**Howie Green:** I have been approached twice by companies wanting to buy my business. One was a publishing company that wanted me to set up my studio inside their company, which sounded great. After months of talks and negotiations, I walked away because it became apparent to me that some of the people in the company thought my approach was too radical. To this day, I remain professional friends with their president, who still sends me projects to work on. The other was an ad agency that threw a lot of money at me and since they were just around the corner from my studio seemed like a great fit. Nice guys, great clients, lots of money—Yay, me! In the midst of figuring out our relationship, their largest client left and that was the end of that. So, yeah, I just work for myself. Alliances are minefields.

**Holly Gonzalez** and I were colleagues at the Boston public relations firm where I had my last nine-to-five job. She later returned to her home state of Florida and started a freelance copywriting business in 1992. Holly now lives and works in Austin, Texas.

Here she recounts her own experience with a partnership gone awry and offers advice on how to avoid such disasters: It seemed like a good idea at the time. Isn't that how so many relationships gone wrong begin?

A little backstory: Lisa and I shared a history. At different points in each of our careers, we had both worked for Shari, a demanding, but hugely talented public relations executive. Shari introduced us to each other, and we bonded instantly. It was a badge of honor that we had survived Shari's, shall we say, "interesting" managerial style. We swapped war stories, but importantly, we became trusted friends and business confidantes. Lisa had launched a small PR firm of her own, while I focused my energies on freelance copywriting, with the occasional event management project. As we were growing our creative businesses at the same time, it was terrific to have someone to talk about the nuts and bolts of clients, contracts, and keeping sane.

I maintained a home office, while Lisa leased office space. She relied on college interns and entry-level account executives to help manage her workload, but she soon realized the need to beef up her staff with a more senior PR professional. When she asked if I'd be willing to work for her part time, I was thrilled. In my fantasy, I would just swing by the office, churn out a few press releases, spiff up a couple of editorial calendars, and be out the door by lunch. Really, how hard could this be?

What I somehow failed to take into account was that while I was on Lisa's dime, I really couldn't call clients, work on my own projects, or schedule meetings. I know, this seems like a no-brainer. But I figured I could tackle some writing before I headed into her office, and return calls and e-mails in the afternoon. And that's what I did, but it wasn't easy, and I sure wasn't happy. For someone who prides herself on responsiveness and quick turnaround, I was failing miserably. I had this tiny window of time when I could meet face-to-face with clients, and I ended up missing vendor and customer calls and scrambling to make deadlines. It was stressful, and my clients got the raw end of the deal.

However, Lisa was appreciative of the skills I brought to the table, and when she laid out her future plans, she wanted me as her vice president and eventual partner in the agency. I will admit that the idea of a steady paycheck, rather than scratching around for new business, was particularly alluring to me.

So I made the decision to scale back my own business and stepped up to manage the agency and its clients, freeing Lisa to focus on drumming up new business. But as I spent more and more time in the office (and less and less time nurturing my own freelance projects), I discovered that while Lisa wanted—and needed—someone like me with solid experience, she wasn't really ready to let go of the reins, leaving me with little flexibility to make decisions, interact with clients, and manage her small staff. So my hours in her office were less than productive, since she needed to sign off on every memo, rewrite every press release, and second-guess every decision. What I should have recognized as red flags I instead brushed off as bumps in the road.

I began to sense some tension and could feel Lisa pulling away—our meetings became less frequent, I was working on fewer projects, and it was hard to actually meet with her, since she seemed to be unavailable—even when she *was* in the office. We had been working on a community relations project for months, and when the client decided not to renew, that was the final tipping point. Understandably, she was stressed, but I figured we'd roll up our sleeves and find some business to replace the lost revenue. Instead, Lisa told me that our deal was done: with the community relations project gone, there was little work that required my expertise—or my salary.

Here I was, not even five months into this alliance, and it had already gone bust. While I should have seen it coming, I was blindsided . . . and I was scared. I had given my clients the heave-ho, and work was scarce. I would essentially need to start my business from scratch all over again. Looking back, it probably took me nearly a year to build my business back up to where it had been before. It's been more than a decade since this alliance debacle, but that experience taught me some lessons that still serve me well today:

- **Don't let your business lie fallow.**
  I made the mistake of stepping away from a business that I had carefully tended and nurtured. It didn't take long for it to

wither on the vine (let's see how many gardening and farming analogies can I cram in here!). This lesson holds true for any small business—don't let a large, seemingly lucrative project take your attention away from your other customers. It can take a minute to lose them, and months, if not years, to get them back, if at all.

- **Be wary of alliances with friends.**

   Sure, there are plenty that work out swimmingly. But in my case, because we were friends, I chose to ignore some clear signs that our arrangement was headed for disaster. Take a minute to consider if you would still partner with this person if they *weren't* your friend. Are your work styles compatible and do they complement one another? Do you see eye-to-eye on critical business decisions? And do each of you respect the other, and trust the other person's judgment?

- **Be true to yourself.**

   I'm a solopreneur. I love that I work for myself, call all the shots, and can choose to work on those projects for which I'm best suited. And I entered into an alliance that squashed the very freedom and independence that I relish. It's no wonder it was doomed to fail! Before you choose to partner up with someone, ask yourself if you'll still be "you."

- **Listen to your gut.**

   Even when the contract looks great on paper and the alliance seems like a winner for all involved, sometimes there's a small nagging voice that's telling you, um, maybe not. What that voice is saying may not be logical, or grounded in reason, but listen to it. Because every business alliance is still a relationship, and if you sense that you're not going to click, talk openly and honestly about your concerns with your prospective partner before you take that leap.

# CHAPTER TWENTY-FIVE

# Avoiding Burnout

My first try at self-employment came in the spring of 1984, when I started doing freelance public relations in Boston. At the time, I lived in a one-bedroom condo, and my desk was immediately beside my bed. During the year and a half I worked on my own, I didn't turn down any work. When the phone rang, I answered and took the project on, no matter how busy I already was. Who knew if the phone would ever ring again? Such is the mind-set of someone just starting out in the world of self-employment. Nothing scares you more than the thought of a long dry spell without any new business.

Taking everything that came my way may have been necessary at the beginning, but by the time my business was really rolling at the end of the first year, the outcome was inevitable: I burned out. There was a two-month period where I worked seven days a week every week. And it was not unusual for me to go to bed only to be unable to sleep because my mind was whirling with work issues. Next thing you'd know, I'd be sitting at that desk tapping those computer keys. Although sitting at a desk and writing from dawn to dusk may not seem like something that would exhaust you, it is very mentally draining if you do it day after day with little or no time for any R&R.

The burnout I suffered led me to make a serious mistake. I was offered that position at a PR firm that I talked about in the introduction, and I took it, less because it was a good opportunity and more because the notion of working regular hours five days a week was mighty appealing. (Of course, things are never what they seem; that job ended up involving plenty of evenings and even some weekends when I had to go to public meetings on behalf of real estate clients or to help manage client-sponsored events.)

## Starting Over with a New Approach

I lasted three years before deciding that, yes, I really had been *far* happier being my own boss and, yes, I had been *far* happier devoting my days to writing than I was filling the management role I'd fallen into at the PR agency. So I quit my job, and as I launched out on my own again, I was determined to do things differently this time around. I was going to avoid burnout at all costs. This meant learning when and how to say no to new projects or new clients and having the discipline necessary to stay out of my office on the weekends and avoiding late night writing binges. (By this time I had moved to a larger condo in a community south of Boston, so avoiding my computer on Saturdays and Sundays was easier than when it was right beside my bed; I could just shut the door to my office.)

Now, this is not to say that I haven't worked plenty of evenings and Saturdays or even Sundays since then. I have, but for the most part, when I've worked that type of schedule it's been because I was tackling something that really excited me—something that would take my career to the next level.

For example, when I worked on the first book I coauthored, I put in plenty of hours on weekends and in the evenings. But that was because I knew having my name on the cover of a book would open up a whole world of ghostwriting opportunities, which it did.

Over the years, I've seen many other self-employed people fall into the same trap I did back in 1984–1986. They work themselves to death for fear that if they take their foot off the pedal for even a few days, it will be the kiss of death for their business. Or they don't have the courage to tell a client that they can't work miracles to meet an unreasonable deadline.

Here's my message to you: If you're burned out, you're no good to your clients, to yourself, or to those you love. Taking on more work than you can handle, twisting yourself into knots to meet unreasonable deadlines, running scared all of the time . . . none of this will help you build a long-lasting, rewarding, and enjoyable career as your own boss.

If your plate is really heaping, know when to turn down new work. Of course, if something really is an emergency situation for a valued client, feel free to take it on. But don't make a habit of this because burnout will be right around the corner. Learn how to pace yourself. Definitely declare at least one day a week as totally work-free, and, yes, that means no checking e-mail. Unless I need to check a movie time or a restaurant menu, I rarely power up my computer on Sundays, for example. And if you're enjoying a vacation or a staycation, enjoy it! Don't be answering e-mail and voice mail. Just step away from that cell phone. Really, the world can go on without you for a few days while you get some much-needed—and much-deserved—R&R.

## Coping Strategies

- **Think before saying "yes."** Besides the keen interest in getting new clients and retaining existing clients, many of us also have a strong desire to please people by saying "yes" when asked to do something. But don't let this mean that you automatically say yes to every project that comes your way. Take a good look at your calendar first and consider what it will mean if you add a new project to an already full calendar. In other words, make conscious decisions instead of reflexively saying yes to every request.

- **Become adept at negotiating timelines.** Know when to say, "Gosh, that is a really great project, and I'd love to work with you on it, but I couldn't start for two more weeks. Would that fit your schedule?" If you've built a strong relationship with a client, they'll understand when you occasionally have to delay a bit before starting something new.

  Similarly, perhaps you can start a project right away but won't be able to finish it within the time span proposed by the client or prospect. Often times, clients have no real idea what a project may involve, so it's up to you to educate them. Show them a realistic timeline that includes all the steps you'll have to take along the way. Unless some emergency has arisen that makes a short timeline imperative, you should be able to negotiate something that doesn't require you to work night and day to get the work done.

- **Become really good at knowing how long a project will take.** One major reason why some people are always overfilling their schedules, I'm convinced, is because they don't have a solid sense of how long projects will take. I'm rarely off by more than 10 percent on my time estimates for projects, and when I am off on my estimate, I almost always have overestimated rather than underestimated. This ability takes time to acquire, but acquire it you must. Without this ability, you'll find yourself overworked—not to mention underpaid if you're consistently underestimating your time on projects that involve agreeing on a flat fee in advance.

- **Develop work calendars for clients to anticipate projects and avoid emergencies.** For example, in my field, we develop marketing calendars that outline the work that will be done in the next three, six, or even twelve months. The client conversation that is involved in developing such a plan will enable you to actually schedule work on a timely basis as you move through the calendar. It will also help avoid those emergency calls when, for example, a client realizes at a late date that they need you to help prepare them for a big upcoming event that they neglected to warn you about.

- **Ditch clients who *only* have emergency projects.** We've all had clients who are always in panic mode and want you to be too. They simply aren't good at planning ahead, so everything they do is done in fire drill mode. I would highly encourage you to avoid such chaos. You can never do your best work under such circumstances, and the stress simply is not worth it.

## ✐ Other Voices ✐

**Stefan Lindegaard:** Some thoughts on avoiding burnout: Two of the great benefits of being self-employed are that you can choose what you do (this brings passion into the equation, which makes so many things easier) and you get flexibility. You can work harder with these two benefits in your work life, but you still have to take the breaks. No one can work at high speed and high quality forever—even on things you love to do. There is a reason that athletes have downtime before peak time. The same goes with productive employees and entrepreneurs.

**Mark G. Auerbach:** Fatigue or burnout can destroy your work output and the quality of your work. I give myself minibreaks during the day. I make a morning coffee date with a friend or colleague to break the monotony of working in my home office. In the summer, I start work earlier, and break for an hour by the pool in the sun. A half hour away from the routine can be restorative. I also make sure I stop doing work at a certain time each day . . . no "check e-mail before bed" for me, or I'd be back at work inadvertently.

**Barbara Rodriguez:** Burnout for me is very mental and psychological. But it also takes its toll physically. I found that meditation helped me to control the stress and helped me to think creatively. I took a course in TM, or transcendental meditation. I sometimes had a problem and could see no way out, but when I meditated, I thought of creative ways to solve problems. I was very surprised. It works!

**Howie Green:** Long ago, I found that I always work best under stress and tight deadlines, but I always had an outlet in my painting pursuits. From my early art school days continuing through today, I paint and draw every day. It has given me a window into other possibilities and other projects. I can be in the middle of an annual report on a crunching deadline and get an idea for a painting. I will do a quick sketch, and just that brief period of time to do the sketch will be a huge relief and get me excited to do the painting . . . then get back to work but with a renewed excitement for a new project.

CHAPTER TWENTY-SIX

# Falling into the Doldrums

When you first launch yourself into self-employment, everything is fresh and exciting. You're constantly learning about running a successful business, and you're meeting lots of new and interesting people as you build your network of contacts. The chances of being bored by your daily routine are slim because it has not actually yet become routine.

This aura of newness and excitement can hang around for quite some time, but sooner or later, things are almost certain to change. You may find yourself slightly bored and hankering for change or for a new challenge. It may take five or ten years or even longer, but it is not unusual to fall into a period where you look ahead and wonder if you can or even desire to keep doing what you're doing for the rest of your career. Welcome to the self-employment doldrums.

I personally hit the doldrums when I had been in business for ten years. Having started my business at the beginning of a recession, the first several years were extremely challenging. As the economy picked up, my business grew quickly; learning how to balance all my new clients' needs was enough of a challenge to keep me interested. Then the Internet came along, and a whole new line of business—writing websites and eventually blogs—opened up for me. A new world of potential clients also opened up since, with the Internet, I could now work with anyone, anywhere; I was soon getting new business queries from other states and even other countries.

## Craving New Challenges

But by 1999, I knew I needed a new intellectual challenge because the thought of spending another decade doing the same stuff over and over again was causing my eyes to glaze over. I decided to take on the challenge of ghostwriting books, which gave me a whole new process to master. Writing two-page press releases and twelve-page brochures was one thing; researching, organizing, and writing an entire book was something entirely new and different. This addition to my repertoire proved to be just the lift I needed to sail out of the doldrums.

Each step of this new adventure presented a challenge. Sometimes, I surely thought I'd bitten off more than I could chew, but when a FedEx delivery person dropped off the first copy of my first coauthored book at my doorstep, I felt a professional thrill unlike anything I'd ever experienced before.

If you're in the doldrums, try what I did and consider how you could expand your services to take your business in a new direction, one that will pique your interest, provide an intellectual challenge, broaden your abilities, and open up new opportunities. Or try these additional strategies.

## Coping Strategies

- **Get away on a long vacation.** Sounds simple, but far too many self-employed people don't take long vacations or sometimes even any vacations. Taking shorter and shorter vacations has been a trend among Americans for some decades now. Despite the fact that having the ability to set your own schedule is one of the biggest attractions of being self-employed, I hear time after time from self-employed people that they just can't get away. The reality is that you can make a vacation happen if you want to, so just do it!

  Personal experience has shown me that going to another locale, hopefully someplace delightful like Europe or the Caribbean, is just what I need to get reenergized. Projects—or people—that seemed tiresome when I left feel more manageable when I return.

  Americans make fun of Europeans for the many weeks of vacation they have each year, but having one's nose stuck to the grindstone year-round can leave us mentally drained and feeling either bored with or exhausted by our work. Health researchers have concluded that *not* taking vacations negatively affects our health to the point that it increases our risk of premature death by *at least 20 percent*.

The trend toward taking mini-vacations doesn't help. You need a minimum of a week away, and preferably two, to fully recharge your batteries. And don't take your clients with you; tell them you won't be answering e-mails, texts, or phone calls while you're away—and then stick to it. You're not really on vacation if you're checking your cell phone constantly.

If the thought of telling your clients that you'll be away for a couple weeks is daunting, ask yourself this: Do your clients go on vacation? Of course they do! And they don't ask if it's okay with you if they do that, do they? No, they just announce that they're going to be gone. There is a real danger in thinking that you're indispensable, for this traps you into thinking you can't get away, when the reality is that for your own well-being, you can't afford not to get away from time to time.

- **Reengage.** For most people, the early years of their business are a time of constant networking. You're out and about all the time, meeting new people to promote your business. Once you've been at it for a number of years, it's easy to let networking fall by the wayside, especially if you've established a solid roster of ongoing clients and aren't particularly looking for new business opportunities. However, those networking activities that you've spurned can also add interest and stimulation to your week. And they provide opportunities to give back through volunteering to serve on committees and boards. Such community service can add meaning to your life and may be just what you need to pull out of the doldrums.

- **Reassess.** Nowhere is it written that you have to keep doing what you're doing forever. Take time to reassess whether your business is really working for you. And I don't mean just whether you're making enough money. Are you truly happy and engaged? Do you actually like what you're doing and the clients with whom you're working? Is it still challenging and meaningful to you?

If the answers to any or all of those questions is "no," how can you fix it? For example, if you're working at home, might you be happier working in a coworking space where there's more interaction with others on a daily basis? And if you can't fix it, what else might you consider doing? Self-employment is great, but as I've written before, it is not for everyone. Maybe it's time to consider a new path.

## ✐ Other Voices ✐

**Stefan Lindegaard:** The pursuit of newness—the search for new things to do and new challenges—can be damaging for the business side of self-employment. I have too many ideas, and there are too many things to explore. This hurts my ability to focus and turn a few strong pieces of my offerings into real products and services that can be sold over and over again. Maybe I don't do this because it becomes tedious and borderline boring. But it might be better for the business if I weren't always coming up with new ideas.

**Pat Mullaly:** Thankfully my business as a graphic designer has a built-in challenge that always keeps me on my toes: technology upgrades! No sooner have I begun to understand a software's capabilities when the designers come up with new tweaks and editions that bring me back to the classroom. Back in the mid-1980s, I used to have to travel an hour each way from my home office to Harvard Square just to set a paragraph of type! Then laser printers were invented and setting type on my Mac was not only doable, it was fun! Aldus PageMaker became Adobe PageMaker, Photoshop and Freehand were introduced, PageMill and GoLive Web Design evolved into Dreamweaver, and QuarkXPress tried to knock them all off the shelf. Keeping up with the latest programs has kept the doldrums from my door.

**Mark G. Auerbach:** I telecommute to work with most of my clients, and we conduct business by e-mail, phone, and Skype. I figured I could telecommute from anywhere, and I have learned to pick up my office and work in warmer winter climates for a couple of weeks at a time. If you plan the face-time meetings carefully, you can turn a mini-vacation and working vacation into one. Start with four to five days away and then build from there. I can work from Florida now for up to three weeks at a stretch.

**Barbara Rodriguez:** I'm at the stage where I want to pursue other interests. I decided to do something related to my business, but something I could control easily and incorporate into my retirement years—something that wouldn't take up my every waking moment. I decided to use my experience to work with community colleges in offering a Medical Interpreting course. I think you can always find something that's related to what you do, but may be more fun, or less stressful, or make you feel like you're giving back. If you take a serious look at yourself, you have many more talents than you give yourself credit for, and those talents can translate into a whole new opportunity. Meditation helps with that creative thinking!

**Howie Green:** Have an outside pursuit and keep it active.

CHAPTER TWENTY-SEVEN

# Getting Discouraged

We all have days—or even weeks—when things just don't go right. If you're self-employed and you run into several of those in a row, you may begin to wonder whether you've chosen the right career path. Discouragement comes knocking, and it's hard not to let him in. This is different from being in the doldrums (i.e., boredom) that I discussed in the previous chapter. What I'm talking about here is being disheartened about how your business is going; it's about fearing that you may have made an unwise career choice and might not have what it takes to succeed in self-employment.

It is very easy to get down in the dumps about how things are going. Perhaps you're in one of those cash flow crises I talked about in chapter 21. Or maybe a big client is being so unreasonably demanding that you're wondering whether you want to continue working together, despite the major hit your income would take if you ended the relationship. Any number of things can be going wrong when you're self-employed, and if several of these things happen at the same time, it can take a toll on your spirit and your enjoyment of your work.

I recall the last time I hit a patch of discouragement. I realized I had underbid on a project and, as a result, would have to eat (i.e., not get paid for) a considerable amount of time. This rarely happens because I've been doing what I do for so long that I'm pretty good at estimating the hours required for a project. But this particular project was a bit unusual, with lots of moving pieces, and I miscalculated. Working for free is not my favorite thing.

We're not talking big money in this case—hundreds of dollars instead of thousands—but any lost income had been very much on my mind at this time since we were in the middle of the Great Recession. In getting ready to do my tax return, I was forced to confront the fact that my income was down significantly from the previous year. I had known as I moved through the year that I wasn't bringing in the usual amount, but until you see that final figure from the end of the year, you always think something will come along to make up the deficit. Alas, nothing did. So I had been in a discouraged state of mind for some weeks.

## Small Annoyances Add Up

At such times, petty aggravations, like my Internet service being down for a day, turn into major irritations. Usually, I take small bumps in the road like this in stride. But as is the case with most people, if I'm already at a low spot mood-wise, the frustration value of everything grows. Even the fact that a client gave me the wrong street number for the office where we were to meet—causing me to drive around a town I wasn't very familiar with looking for a building that didn't exist—seemed outrageous, instead of just something I could laugh off.

I have no magical formula for turning things around at those times when things seem discouraging, but here are coping strategies that have helped me get through such periods.

## Coping Strategies

- **Realize that this, too, shall pass.** Don't let a bad week or even a bad month throw you off your path. It is unrealistic to think that everything will go just swimmingly for your business all the time. (If you talk to someone who is self-employed who tells you they've never had some discouraging times, I venture to say you're talking to a liar.) When you've weathered a few storms, it becomes easier to make it through another one because you then have a history to look back upon. You can tell yourself, "Hey, I made it through that other bad time, so I can make it through this one."

  Then again, if *every* month seems to be a bad month, perhaps you are, in fact, on the wrong path. Don't be afraid to admit it if you fear that's the case. A close examination of just what is going wrong and why may be in order. Fix the things that are within your control—like being sure you bid on jobs correctly—and learn to brush off the things that you can't control . . . like Internet service blips or clients sending you on a wild goose chase for an address that doesn't exist.

- **Have someone to talk to who understands what it means to be self-employed.** The best cure for being discouraged—other than having things start to turn around and go amazingly well—is to have someone to talk things over with. Certainly, many significant others and spouses are adept at serving in this role, but depending on your field of work and how much they understand about it—and about being self-employed— they may not be your best source of good advice. Or they may have heard you whine so often that their eyes automatically glaze over when you start up again about how bad things are for you right now.

  This is why it's good to have two or three confidants who are also self-employed and who know the drill. Going out to lunch with a good listener who has been through the same kinds of stresses and strains as you have and who is also good at providing feedback and advice can be an invaluable way to let off steam—and to gain new insights that will help you turn things around.

- **Don't just sit there; take action.** When you're discouraged, it is all too easy to fall into a real funk that makes it hard to move forward. Navel-gazing is all well and good for helping you determine why things are going wrong, but at some point, you have to draw up a plan and take action. Perhaps you need to change your client base. Maybe there's a new skill you need to add to your repertoire. Whatever change is needed, start getting it done.

# CHAPTER TWENTY-EIGHT

# Feeling All Alone

Being a sole practitioner can be a lonely experience. This seems to be more the case now than it was in 1989 when I started my business. Back then, meetings with clients were far more frequent because we didn't have Internet tools like freeconferencecall.com and gotomeeting.com, which enable us to hold conference calls with people at multiple sites while we all simultaneously view the same material online. (I used to have a weekly marketing call with one client in which there were often people on the line from six different locations and we were all viewing the same page of our marketing schedule via gotomeeting.com.) Now, I sometimes go a month or two without setting foot in any client's office.

I used to make it a practice to try to get out of the house—and thereby away from my home office—at least once a day. But even that habit fell by the wayside when the price of gas rose to a point where going out for a ride every day at noon began to seem wasteful. This was particularly true during the eleven-year-period when I lived in a lovely rural town in western Massachusetts, where anything you'd want to get to—like a coffee shop, a deli, a supermarket, the bank, or the post office—was at least five miles away from my house. Fortunately, by then I was no longer living alone, so the issue of isolation was greatly lessened.

People have become so accustomed to conducting business through e-mail that even the phone doesn't ring nearly as often as it used to. On one hand, that's a good thing because, as a writer, I can do without the interruptions of frequent phone calls. But on the other hand, e-mail is equally intrusive and doesn't produce any real sense of human connection, which the phone at least does. It's difficult to build a personal relationship with a client if your primary means of communication is e-mail.

## Know How Much Aloneness You Can Take

This isolation is one of the reasons self-employment isn't for everybody. If you're someone who isn't comfortable spending long stretches of time alone, then carefully consider making the leap to self-employment, especially if you're going to work from a home office and aren't going to have any employees. Our workdays can be long, and even if you live with someone, consider whether you'll really be happy shut up in your home office alone throughout that long day.

If you'd describe yourself as a "social person" who thrives on being around people, you may have a hard time adjusting to life as a sole practitioner. Also, if you live alone and plan to work at home, consider how you'll cope with this extra degree of isolation. Even if you have a spouse or a significant other, if that person leaves early in the morning to go to work and doesn't reappear until the early evening, that leaves you with a long stretch of time by yourself.

Of course, you can always get out to networking meetings and have coffee or lunch dates with colleagues and friends. But all that is time consuming, and if you're really busy, you may be reluctant to drop everything and go out. But sometimes you really need to. I have two friends with whom I have breakfast from time to time. I sometimes think as I'm going out the door, "I don't have time for this. Why am I going out?" But by the time I get back, I know it was good for my mental health, and I'm more productive the rest of the day because I went out and got some human companionship.

Obviously, not all professions are like mine. Some people who work on their own get to meet with clients all the time. For example, if you're running a home decorating or home staging business, you're going to have plenty of face-to-face interaction with clients in their homes. And there are many other fields where the same thing is true. But if you're taking up one of the many businesses where you're expected to be chained to your computer in your office day in and day out, you may want to carefully figure out strategies for coping with this peril of self-employment.

## Coping Strategies

- **Recognize from the get-go that isolation may be a problem.** It's important to start off acknowledging that, depending on your circumstances, working alone can be isolating. Without this understanding, you may not take steps to cope with the isolation and, as a result, may find yourself becoming dissatisfied or even depressed fairly soon after you become self-employed and wondering why. I always thought I was someone who had no problem with spending long amounts of time alone. But even I found that spending workday after workday all by myself quickly became too much aloneness and adopted my "go out at lunchtime every day" routine.

- **Build real human interaction into your day.** If my observations are correct, it seems that many of the people I know who work alone at home use social media like Facebook to drive off the isolation. This is fine as far as it goes (although it can be a huge time-sucking distraction at times), but it really can't replace talking to real live people.

  Adopt your own version of my former method of going out to do errands every lunchtime. Maybe it's going to the gym. Maybe it's spending an hour at the local coffee shop, plugged into your laptop but still out among people. Try different things and see what works best for you. Just make sure that more days than not you get out there and interact with other people.

- **Get a pet!** The day I started my business, Jasper, a six-week-old kitten, moved into my condo. He was with me for the next nineteen years, providing amusement, comfort, and "someone" to talk to. (He was also a very vocal kitty, so there was someone talking back as well!) Now there's a puggle named Molly and a cat named Cosmo living with me. A dog gives you a reason to get out into your neighborhood a couple times a day, providing more chances for human interaction. Dog walking also brings the added benefit of giving you some exercise—something those of us pursuing sedentary occupations need.

- **Explore options other than working at home, including the growing trend of shared workplaces.** It could be that working alone at home is just not for you. Thankfully, as I mentioned earlier, an increasing number of coworking spaces are available in many places. In such facilities, you can share the overhead of having an office with others while benefitting from having other people around you as you work. And if you're in the very early stages of your business, you may be able to find a space in a small business incubator; again, you'll benefit from low overhead and an environment filled with other people who are at similar stages of business growth. Such a situation may also lead to new business for you among your fellow tenants and among their clients as they get to know you and feel comfortable referring you to others. Some incubators also provide free or low-cost training and mentoring, designed to help you get your business off to a good start. Check with your local community college; many of them have incubator space, but if they don't, they will at least know where such space is available in your community.

---

## ✍ Other Voices ✍

**Stefan Lindegaard:** I am a very introverted person, and I do not like the idea of meeting people in person or even talking on the phone. It is not as bad as it sounds because it is actually more the idea of getting out that is difficult. I tend to enjoy it when I interact with others in the real world, although I can't do too much of it, and I also need substantial downtime afterward. My preferred communication tools are e-mail and social media (LinkedIn and Twitter). It is not the same as real interactions, but they are actually a good substitute or tool for building and nurturing relationships. I have many people whom I have had many good interactions with even though I have never met them in real life.

**Barbara Rodriguez:** Be careful what you wish for. I had a lot of alone time until my spouse retired. Now, I long for alone time. I've had to demand that no one enter my office at certain times of day. I've put notes on the door. I did go through a phase, prior to my spouse's retirement, where I felt very isolated, but it's only because I allowed myself to be at my computer day after day and not socialize. I got myself into a rut, and that's just not me. Going after and winning a customer is one of the most self-satisfying parts of my business. There's nothing like meeting in person. Everyone is communicating electronically these days. If you want something to set you apart, visit your customers. It's so important to put a face with the name. It humanizes you. It helps your business and helps alleviate feelings of isolation.

**Howie Green:** I make sure I book a dinner with a friend or two every week and I go out to the local pool to go swim two to three times a week. It's good to get naked with strangers, get some exercise, and converse with friends face-to-face. It's especially important now when we tend to think of a Facebook comment as a conversation with a friend.

# CHAPTER TWENTY-NINE

# Secondhand Stress

An underlying theme of many of the challenges you'll face when you're self-employed is stress. Most of the stress I've written about so far arises when something happens to you specifically, but I also want to acknowledge that when you're self-employed, you can also feel stress because of what is happening to others. I call this secondhand stress. And much like secondhand smoking, this stress can harm your own well-being and can even affect your income.

Secondhand stress occurs when your clients or customers are under a strain and their distress causes you distress. When you, yourself, are under stress, you can usually do something about the situation to relieve the pressure. But when it's a client who is face-to-face with trouble, there is often very little you can do to help other than to lend an ear and offer advice, much of which is likely to be ignored.

A few times I was gratified to find that a client actually listened to and acted on what I suggested and things took a turn for the better. But that has been rare. Most of the time, people just want a shoulder to cry on, and it's easier for them to pick you to be that person rather than someone within their own organization. I think they do this because often they don't want to admit to anyone in their company that a potential disaster is in the offing. Being a client's favorite confidante seems like it would be easy, but it really isn't, especially at those times when what the client needs to talk about is all bad news.

## Close Bonds Develop

Client relationships can be strong, especially if they have some longevity to them. I have formed very meaningful, caring bonds with a number of clients. I consider this one of the biggest benefits of being self-employed. For the most part, you can pick and choose the people you work for and can avoid people who aren't your cup of tea for some reason. (Okay, not always . . . a bad apple does creep in now and then, but then you can always fire them.)

As a result of this closeness, while the problem your client faces isn't your own, you still may wake up in the middle of the night worrying just as much as if the problem were your own. I spent hours and hours in the 1990s commiserating with a client who had perpetual problems with a series of new partners she had brought into her business. Some months, I probably spent as much, if not more, time listening to her problems than I did doing actual billable work for her! This in itself was pretty frustrating, but it was also a source of worry to know that this client, who I liked and respected a great deal, was not able to grow her business as she wished because she kept picking the wrong partners.

We all want our clients' businesses to thrive because then ours will too. So there is a strong element of self-interest here, obviously. But it goes beyond that. I simply hate to see a client who is under severe stress, especially when I can do little to resolve the issue that is causing the stress. And thus, I sometimes think that secondhand stress is even worse than firsthand stress. My own problems I can solve or at least take action on. But sitting on the sidelines and watching someone you've formed a strong bond with get whacked around by the often-fickle fates of the business world is hard!

Another big potential downside exists when clients share their problems with you. Aside from any sleeplessness that secondhand stress may cause you, you may not get paid for the time you devote to listening to a client's woes. If you are working on a project on a flat-fee basis and the client spends precious meeting or phone call minutes talking about something other than your project, that time still counts against your time budget in the client's mind. The client will not want to hear, "Well, I'm charging you extra because you took a half hour of our project meeting time to discuss your problems." So you'll be stuck eating a lot of unpaid time for clients who make a habit of bringing up non-project-related worries they have.

## Coping Strategies

- **Learn to identify secondhand stress.** It's tremendously helpful to recognize that secondhand stress is a phenomenon that you, too, may encounter if you're self-employed. Without recognizing this condition for what it is and accepting your inability to resolve your clients' problems, you may feel anxious or stressed out without understanding why . . . which could add even more stress. Once the source of your angst is identified, you will be better able to put it out of your mind.

- **Try to refocus discussions with clients.** Learn to steer the conversation back to the client's project sooner rather than later in meetings or phone calls. Yes, you do need to appear sympathetic to the stress the client is feeling, but that doesn't mean you can't take control of the conversation and get it back on topic.

  One effective method for doing this is to have a written agenda for your meetings. This is especially important to do with clients who you've learned through experience have a tendency to get off track. Learn how to say something along the lines of, "I am so sorry you're having this problem. I'd like to think about it for a few days and see if I can come up with ideas that might be helpful. But in the meantime, we need to make some decisions about these agenda items."

  Depending on the nature of your relationship with the client, you may even go so far as to point out that this side discussion is eating into the hours budgeted for their project. Offer to schedule a breakfast or lunch meeting soon where you could focus solely on their problem. This shows you care but also reminds them that you're on the clock and that you therefore need to focus on the project at hand.

- **Set boundaries.** In my experience, the type of client who shares their business (and sometimes personal) problems with you is also the type of client who is apt to call you at any hour of the day or on weekends. This means they'll deliver a nice heap of secondhand stress into your life any time they care to do so. Do not let them interrupt your personal time. For example, I always made it well known to clients that I would never be available on Sundays. I told them that was the one day I didn't turn on my computer or answer my phone.

  Let caller ID be your best friend. Do not feel you must answer evening or weekend calls from clients who you know are likely to be calling to vent on one of their own issues instead of seeking to talk about what you're working on for them. Same with e-mails; do not feel compelled to read or answer them during nonbusiness hours.

  Of course, this advice does not have to be applied universally to all your clients. Some will have legitimate emergencies that need your attention off hours. But over time, you will learn who is likely to be reaching out after hours because they genuinely need your assistance and who just wants someone to listen to their woes.

- **Master relaxation techniques that work for you.** This advice serves not only for relieving secondhand stress but also all the other forms of stress that enter your life when you're self-employed. You need to find one or more relaxation techniques that enable you to put your stress aside. Meditation, yoga, exercise, guided imagery, journaling, doing art or craft projects, gardening . . . the list of possibilities is long. Figure out what works for you and make it a part of your daily life, even in times when you're not feeling stressed. By making stress-relief techniques a habit, you may even find you're less susceptible to having secondhand stress disrupt your sleep or ruin your good mood.

## ✑ Other Voices ✑

**Barbara Rodriguez:** Secondhand stress for me comes from family dramas. I have too much to think about without additional drama, but most of the time it's unavoidable. There are times when I can hear an upsetting conversation in the background and I try to ignore it, but even subliminally, I know that it adds to my stress. It's another thing to think about. You need to protect yourself from that at all costs. It cuts into your day, your ability to think clearly, and your ability to sleep soundly.

**Howie Green:** Secondhand stress is constant. Everyone I know is crazy at one time or another and tries to pass off their nuttiness onto me. I just put up my deflector shields and let it bounce off. Not my circus; not my monkeys.

# CHAPTER THIRTY

# Dealing with Insecurity

I was fortunate to have a mother who encouraged rather than criticized. But the one character flaw she did frequently point out to me was that I was impatient. I wanted things to happen when I wanted them to happen, not on anybody else's timetable.

Alas, all Mother's good advice about learning patience never totally sank in. I'm still impatient, and it shows up when I send a piece of writing off to a client or a proposal to a prospect and don't hear back from them quickly. What's wrong with these people? Isn't this important to them? Aren't we on a schedule here? Why haven't they called me?

Feedback! I need feedback and I need it now! I think I became spoiled in high school when I'd turn in an essay and get it back the next day with a grade. I still need a grade! How am I doing? I need to know!

It finally dawned on me a few years back that what this boils down to is not so much impatience but insecurity. All writers, I think, suffer from some level of self-doubt. No matter how much success we've had or how long we've been doing what we do, we always think that perhaps one day, we'll lose our touch. The skill of writing—or performing any creative act—seems ephemeral, like something that I could wake up one day and find I'd lost overnight. The fact that it's a skill I began mastering in grade school doesn't seem to matter. Somewhere in my brain lurks the idea that it could all go up in smoke someday.

As a result, when I send an article or some web copy off to a client and they don't respond in a timely fashion, I fear they're not responding because they hate what I wrote and are avoiding having to tell me that. The fact that roughly two people in my entire career have ever harshly criticized my writing (and they were people who were terrible writers themselves) doesn't seem to stop this insecurity.

## All Alone with Your Fears

Writers aren't alone, I'm sure, in fretting about whether they may lose their touch at some point. It takes a supremely confident person to go through life without ever worrying about whether one's talent and skills are up to snuff. The problem with this when you're self-employed is that you have no one else to bounce things off of before sending your work out the door to the client . . . no one who can reassure you that the bit of work you've just completed is right on the mark . . . or that it could benefit from just a little more tweaking. So you need some coping strategies for when you break out into a cold sweat over a project.

## Coping Strategies

- **Get a reliable sounding board.** It is possible to find a colleague who can help with this problem. For example, I have a relationship with a colleague in which we each ask the other to edit our work from time to time. This boosts our confidence when we finally do send something off to a client, and it gives the client the benefit of having two sets of professional eyes look at a piece of writing. Although we are dear friends, we keep this part of our relationship professional by charging each other for our time. This ensures that neither of us will feel imposed upon if one of us needs a lot more of this type of assistance than the other one does during a given time period. In other words, don't ask a friend to give you feedback for free; if you do, you'll soon wear out your welcome.
- **Stay on top of the latest in your field.** There are few fields in which new things aren't popping up quite often. For example, I've had to learn about social media over the past decade. But between the pressure of serving your existing clients, working to attract new clients, and trying to have some work/life balance, it can be easy to fall behind the pace of change in your field. This will inevitably produce insecurity when clients start asking you whether you can handle the new things that have popped up. Sooner or later, every self-employed person finds himself or herself saying yes to a client request that involves something new while

silently wondering, "I have no idea how to do that." It's happened to me more than once. Cue the panic attack music.

Regularly setting aside time to keep up with new trends and learn how they will impact the services you need to provide to keep clients happy is much better than trying to learn new things on the run to keep clients happy. Knowing you're up-to-date on the latest developments will boost your confidence. Plus, as a bonus, instead of waiting for clients to request services related to the latest developments, you can be the one to bring up the idea in client conversations.

- **Remember that you're not always top of mind with clients.** Over the years I've learned that there are many, many reasons why clients or prospects don't respond as quickly as I'd like. Most of these reasons have absolutely nothing to do with the project we're working on or how they feel about my work or about my proposal. So in more recent years I have learned patience to a much greater degree. Mother would be so proud. Now if only I could totally conquer the insecurity.

---

### ✐ Other Voices ✐

**Howie Green:** For creative types like me, insecurity is just a way of life. There is always someone out there doing stuff better than you or someone who you wish you were . . . it's just part of the culture, and you can't let it get to you. I have seen many of my peers fall by the wayside due to their struggle with insecurity. Hey, some days you're great, and some days you're just okay. Even Monet had to paint the same thing multiple times to get it right.

# CHAPTER THIRTY-ONE

# Bonus Chapter

## Eight Behaviors to Avoid If You're Self-Employed

Perils from the outside, such as a faltering economy, disloyal clients, or feckless alliance partners, are not the only challenges self-employed people face. As Walt Kelly's comic strip star Pogo said, "We have met the enemy, and he is us." All too often, it is your own behaviors that will get you in trouble. This bonus chapter covers eight behaviors, attitudes, or habits that you should strive to avoid when you're your own boss. I've mentioned some of these issues tangentially before, but they're of such importance that I thought they deserved more thorough attention here.

### #1: Analysis Paralysis

Analysis paralysis—in which you put off an important decision until you have every last bit of information in your hands—is an extremely common phenomenon throughout the business world . . . and beyond, of course. I've witnessed this inability to pull the trigger on decisions both large and trivial in a timely way everywhere from large corporations to one-person businesses.

For someone who is self-employed, analysis paralysis can bring your forward momentum to a grinding halt. The longer you spend gathering every last snippet of data before deciding how to move forward with your marketing or whatever it is you're dithering about, the longer you will spend spinning your wheels in the status quo. Here are ideas to consider when you find yourself unable to make a move because you're suffering from analysis paralysis.

- **Risk is inherent in any business.** Whether it's a giant corporation trying to decide whether to risk millions on a new product line or a tiny little company that is unable to decide whether to spend a portion of its small marketing budget on a new strategy, it's important to realize that you're going to win some and lose some. Nobody bats a thousand. The key thing is to be in the game, not on the sidelines endlessly going through your playbook trying to find a guaranteed-to-win strategy.

- **Not deciding is deciding.** I'm a pretty decisive person, but there are times when I just can't make a choice. Then, I remind myself that by delaying, I actually *am* making a choice . . . a choice not to move ahead. The longer you wait, the greater chance there is that the window of opportunity you originally saw will close up as competitors who are more nimble decision makers move ahead. There may be a cost in delaying, and in some cases, it can be considerable.

- **You will probably never have every last bit of information you need.** Once a month on my blog, I put together a post that is a compendium of business advice. The more of these I've written, the more I've begun to wonder about all the information that is now available at the touch of a keyboard to solopreneurs and small business owners. Undoubtedly, some people—the really analytical ones or those for whom making decisions is naturally difficult—get bogged down in chasing after every bit of information out there. When you read enough blog posts, you're bound to come across conflicting advice and then what do you do? You probably go off searching for yet more input. Is this really productive? (And yes, I *do* realize that for someone writing an advice blog, there is probably some irony in these reflections since I'm just adding to the possibility of information overload.)

- **No one's opinion counts more than yours.** I have had clients who have kept saying, "I just want to have one more person look at this before I decide." And then when that one more person has looked at it, they suddenly remember yet someone else whose opinion they must have before moving ahead.

  I'm not saying you shouldn't check with trusted advisers. But at some point, this gets ridiculous. If ten people have told you it's a good idea—or a lousy idea—should that eleventh person's opinion really make all the difference in what you decide?

  During various administrations in Washington, I've heard people describe how a president has made decisions by saying that he "listens to the last person in the room," meaning that the last person to talk to the president is the one who holds sway over the policy direction taken.

That, of course, is a horrible way to make important decisions. Don't let this be you. Whether you're a solopreneur or running a small business with employees, you have the most to win or the most to lose. It's your opinion that counts.

- **Learn to trust your gut.** When the research you've done conflicts and the people around you are divided over an issue, it's sometimes necessary to go with your intuition. It won't always be right, but if you have solid experience and have done a reasonable amount of research, you're probably not going to drive your business off a cliff by deciding to go with your gut on something.

  To build your faith in your intuition, try to make note of the many small and correct decisions you constantly make based on nothing more than your instincts. This will give you faith that you can do the same when it comes to making bigger, more impactful choices.

- **Above all, be alert for symptoms of analysis paralysis.** When you've asked a lot of people for input and find yourself thinking that you should ask just a few more, recognize that you may be in the grip of analysis paralysis. If you find yourself sitting up at night poring over the data for the umpteenth time, know that you need to stop analyzing and start deciding.

  It helps to set deadlines for making decisions. And let others know of these deadlines, so you can't just keep pushing it back without having to explain why you're doing so. And if you do push a deadline back, make sure you have a darn good reason for it.

  Analysis paralysis can be a life-threatening disease for any business. The business world is so competitive and moving so fast that we all have to be as nimble and agile as possible. Sometimes deciding to do nothing is the best choice, but make sure that it is a conscious decision and not just a result of analysis paralysis.

## #2: Living in the Past

When you're self-employed, you cannot afford to live in the past or cling to the status quo. If you are resistant to change, it can cause you to ignore warning signs that the environment in which you operate is shifting and that you need to change with it. More innovative and agile competitors will take advantage of these changing conditions and leave you in the dust.

If you're bound up with preserving the way you have always done things in your business, you assume you can accurately predict future events based on prior outcomes without considering that changing conditions may produce new outcomes. If you are the type of person who is fond of saying things like "We tried that before and it didn't work" or "We've always done it this other way and it works just fine," then you are clinging to conventional thinking. You fail to recognize that changing conditions may mean that an idea tried before will now work or that the old way of doing things is no longer adequate.

You cling to the status quo when you:

- **Fail to keep track of trends affecting your business.** The examples of companies that have gone out of business because they didn't continue to innovate to serve the shifting needs of their customers are legion.
- **Do not set and track proper success metrics that will alert you to warning signs that things need to change.** Do you even know what metrics you should be tracking? This is one of those tasks that can very easily fall through the cracks when you're self-employed and trying to devote every hour to bringing in income. Figure out what metrics you should be measuring and make it a practice to check how you're doing against these measures at least once a month.
- **Believe you can ignore warning signs that indicate a change is needed.** Sometimes even when small business owners are measuring the right things, they refuse to accept that downward trends are meaningful and lasting until they're too deep in a hole to recover. While I believe being optimistic is almost essential to being self-employed, you do have to take off those rose-colored glasses now and then to make sure you're seeing conditions as they really are.

Your view of the status quo and why it must be maintained is based on beliefs you have established throughout your career, including while you've been self-employed. The problem comes when we fail to challenge these beliefs in view of altered market conditions. But challenge them you must if you hope to keep up with the rapidly shifting market conditions that we all face these days.

## Magical Thinking

When I hear my solopreneur and small business clients talk about their glorious past successes and hear their assurances that the bad things that are happening to them now will soon work themselves out, I think of the title of Joan Didion's memoir, *The Year of Magical Thinking*. Magical thinking is holding beliefs that cannot be justified by observation or reason. To move into the future requires clearheaded decision-making that isn't distorted by memories of how great things used to be. If everything were still working just fine, then would your sales look increasingly anemic? Would you be losing customers to a new competitor? Would your debt be mounting?

When it comes to evaluating how well your business is doing and making decisions about its future, you can't afford to live in the past. Business today changes at a faster pace than ever. Those who lag behind—clinging to outdated modes of operation and refusing to veer from what brought them success in the first place—are not on the path to long-term success. They're living in a land of magical thinking, a place where you definitely do not want to take up residence.

### Change Is Scary, But Necessary

I know all too well that change makes many, many people nervous. Countless times I've presented a new marketing strategy to a client—often one that was struggling with flat or even declining sales—only to have the idea rejected in favor of their "tried and true" strategies, despite the fact that those were no longer working. I've often had to bite my tongue to keep from saying, "Why don't you try to bury your head a little deeper in that sand you've got it stuck in?"

It has always been amazing to me just how bad some solopreneurs and small business owners are willing to let things get before they will pull themselves out of the past and decide to give something new a go. I've often heard some version of this statement: "This is just a short turndown; I'm sure things will pick up soon if we just keep plugging away as usual."

Yes, change may make you nervous. Yet the ability to figure out when changes are needed and to follow through will be critical to your long-term success. When you're making decisions, stop and ask yourself if your underlying assumptions are really accurate . . . or are you making choices based on your fear of change. Do you have up-to-date data and research to back up your decisions or are you just basing your decision on past experience without checking to see if that experience is still valid under today's conditions?

If you have employees, breed a culture in which people are encouraged to question the status quo instead of being punished for doing so, as happens in far too many organizations. The result will be better decision-making and a stronger business.

## #3: Perfectionism

Okay, okay, I can already hear the perfectionists in the audience shouting, "What's wrong with being a perfectionist? I'm proud to be a perfectionist!" Well, there's plenty wrong with it. When you can't let go of something until it's perfect, you'll procrastinate, perhaps face cost overruns, and may not satisfy the client because you're so late with your delivery. What good is something to a client if it is perfect but gets there too late to be of help or actually causes problems with the firm's own operations? In general, clients don't like vendors—no matter how great their work is—who cause them heart palpitations by constantly pushing up against, or even past, deadlines.

There's also another problem with perfectionism. If you're fussing over every single detail of a project, you will tend to make things more complicated than they need to be. Perfectionists overanalyze, overthink, and, in general, overdo everything. When you're so wrapped up in the minutiae of a project, it's very likely that you'll lose sight of the big picture.

If you have staff members, your perfectionism will drive them nuts as you try to micromanage every aspect of their work. It can be especially damaging if you have senior people with considerable experience who don't really need or want you looking over their shoulder constantly. This control-freak attitude was high on the lists of reasons I left my last nine-to-five job.

Another downside of perfectionism is that you may end up working hours for which you will not be paid. If you have given a client a fixed budget for a project but continue to work beyond the hours that budget calls for, you will in essence be working for free during those extra hours. For this reason, make sure you're tracking your hours carefully. If you see that you're in danger of putting in time for which you will not be paid, this signals that either you didn't set the budget correctly or, more likely, your perfectionism is getting in your way. This is not to say that sometimes running a little over budget is not justifiable; that happens to all of us from time to time. But if you do this constantly, take a good look in the mirror and see if you're not looking at someone who needs to dial back on his/her perfectionist streak.

Even if you don't have a budget cap and can bill every hour you work, this may end up with a final total cost that is not pleasing to the client. Next time they have a similar project, they may look for a more affordable solution. In other words, your perfectionism may price you out of the market.

Perhaps worst of all, your ability to grow your business can be seriously stymied if you are a perfectionist. You may spend so much time completing each and every task that you have no time to devote to innovating new product offerings, to attracting new clients for your services, or other activities that will support business growth.

### Not Advocating Sloppiness

Obviously, I am not arguing in favor of being slipshod. We all take pride in our work and want to do a good job for those who buy our products or services. But there does come a point in every project where the law of diminishing returns kicks in and you need to recognize when the amount of difference you're making by seeking perfection simply won't be meaningful enough to your end user to justify the effort.

For example, every time I pick up one of the books I've written, I can quickly find something that I'd like to revise. But I long ago accepted that writers are never truly satisfied. So when it's time to turn over a manuscript, I don't fret that if I had time to do one more draft, I would have a perfect book. Because, by this time, I know no book is ever perfect.

And perhaps that is the biggest downside of perfectionism. If you constantly strive to be perfect and to do everything perfectly, you may never be truly satisfied with anything, no matter how much hard work you put into it and how pleased your client is. Instead, live by this motto: "Always do your best," recognizing that on some days your best will be truly fabulous and on other days it will just be good, but it is still the best you have to offer the world on that day. That is really all anyone—including ourselves—can expect from us.

## #4: Clinging to Your Comfort Zone

A few years ago, I had a conversation with a friend about a potential project I was hoping to pass along to her. She told me she had thought about the assignment—ghostwriting a book—and decided it was "outside her comfort zone." Now, she had several valid reasons for not wanting to take on a new project right then, including family issues and an imminent move. But not being willing to step outside her comfort zone to try something new that would significantly expand the potential of her business seems to me to be an all too common mistake among many self-employed people and small business owners.

This was only one of many instances I've seen of friends and colleagues who were not willing to try something new. They cling to what they know, even when what they know isn't working very well for them. They're certain that if they just keep beating that dead horse long enough, things will turn around. Or, if things are going okay, they still hesitate to try something that may make things even better. They stay in their comfort zone, unwilling to take a risk, even if a risk/reward analysis would show them that the risk is relatively little and the potential reward is significant.

Certainly, when I first thought about taking on book-length ghostwriting projects, the idea was daunting. Could I really do this? Could I write a whole book, given that the longest piece I'd previously written was my master's thesis? While the idea made me nervous, at the same time continuing to stick with short writing projects that I'd always done was not an inviting prospect. It was time for something new, so I crawled out on that limb. Luckily, the limb held, and I found myself with a new skill that has been both intellectually and financially rewarding.

### Go Ahead, Take a Risk

My question to you is this: Do you want to live your whole career inside your comfort zone? I realize everyone has different levels of risk tolerance based on the financial demands of their lives. And if you're totally happy and your financial needs are being met by staying within your current comfort zone, then you may have little motivation to try something new and different. But if you do step outside that zone and succeed, you will find that great satisfaction comes from conquering your fears and expanding your comfort zone.

I respected my friend's decision not to proceed because I knew that her life was extremely hectic at that point and the timing was probably not right for this particular project. But what I wanted to say to her is that your comfort zone is not a static thing. It can change and grow, and as it grows, so do you. So the next time you find yourself turning down an opportunity because it is outside your comfort zone, first carefully consider whether your comfort zone isn't really more of a trap than something that brings you comfort.

## #5: Frequent Second-Guessing

Long ago I had a boss who made a habit of rethinking decisions that had already been made. Man, does that get tiresome fast! A staff meeting that began with "I think we need to revisit (insert decision made at last week's staff meeting here)" brought a desire to pound your head on the table because the pain of doing that would be less than having to rehash, yet again, what everyone at the table thought was settled business.

Second-guessing decisions and frequently backtracking or switching directions can be highly detrimental to your business. Here's how:

- **Subcontractors and vendors may never totally commit to a strategy because they know it might be abandoned shortly.** When discussing new marketing plans with client companies, I have sometimes sensed indifference or skepticism from staff members who will be charged with implementing pieces of the plan. Upon probing, it's been clear that these attitudes are based on the fact that this is a "plan of the month" company. I've even had people use exactly those words to describe what life is like at their workplace. You can hardly blame them for their lack of enthusiasm.

When changes in direction are frequent, nothing new ever gets fully embraced because your colleagues think it's unlikely to last. If a subcontractor sometimes doesn't move forward with an assignment and when asked says something along the lines of "Oh, I wasn't sure you were serious about that," it may be a sign that you change directions so frequently that people aren't sure they're ever on solid ground with a project.

- **Strategies and plans with real potential are never given a full chance to succeed.** If the slightest resistance is felt or things don't go 100 percent according to plan right out of the gate, everything gets tossed overboard and it's back to the drawing board. This ignores the fact that very few things ever go perfectly. Success is never guaranteed, but good ideas that have been thoroughly researched and planned are worth giving time to prove themselves. Sure, tweaking needs to be done more often than not, but that's far different from second-guessing yourself and abandoning something before it's been given a real chance to make an impact.
- **Customers can also become confused as to what your business is really about.** Customers don't like frequent changes in direction from their vendors. Puzzling shifts in policies that affect customers, marketing messages that change so often they create confusion, initiatives that are announced and then shortly abandoned—all of these things can cause customers to wonder if you really know what you're doing.

The root of such indecision, of course, is self-doubt. This is possibly a more common problem among newly self-employed people than among those with more experience who have learned to trust their own judgment. But it's also possible to find some freelancers who have been around for a while who suffer from deep-seated insecurity that causes them to constantly revisit decisions.

The next time you feel the urge to revisit a decision, stop and think about the impact this bad habit is having on your business. Do you really need to revisit a decision, or do you just need to tweak things a little bit? Are the reasons you made the decision in the first place still valid? Did you make the decision based on good input from subcontractors, customers, mentors, and business advisers? Has something really changed that makes the decision suddenly invalid, or are you just feeling insecure because things aren't going absolutely according to plan? Have you given the decision enough time to work, or are you in danger of pulling the plug prematurely on what is still an essentially good idea? Consider these questions carefully before changing directions yet again.

## #6: Self-Doubt and Fear

While glued to the TV watching *The Roosevelts* on PBS in 2014, I was struck by how many times Eleanor Roosevelt expressed self-doubt and fear about whether she was up to the task ahead of her. It reminded me of reading my mother's college diaries, which I found among her papers after she died in 1981. My mother taught high school English for more than thirty years and was much loved by her pupils. To this day, I still hear from former students who say she was their favorite teacher. Yet in the diary she wrote while student teaching, she expressed great doubt about whether she was up to the job of teaching high school students.

Does self-doubt or fear keep you in an unrewarding nine-to-five job when what you'd really like to do is to become self-employed or start a small business? If you're already self-employed, do you have countless logical-sounding reasons (i.e., excuses) as to why you can't make that next move forward that would take your business to a whole new level?

For example, do you delay implementing an idea that would take you and your business in a new direction because "the timing just isn't right?" The real reason that frequently underlies this and other things that slow us down—like the analysis paralysis that I mentioned earlier—may be that you doubt your ability to do what needs to be done. You fear the unknown and you fear failure because you're not sure you're up to the job.

Very few of us don't have some degree of self-doubt. Certainly, not all nuclear families do a good job of nurturing self-confidence in their offspring. It was clear from Eleanor Roosevelt's childhood, as portrayed by Ken Burns, that she had few people in her life who would build her up and tell her she could succeed. (And she had the added disadvantage of being born in a time when women were not expected to achieve much beyond getting married and having children.) And yet, as her example shows, it is possible to overcome self-doubt ingrained in us as children and move forward—even shining as Mrs. Roosevelt did as she grew into one of the most respected and even transformative figures of the twentieth century.

The next time you come up with a dozen excuses for not tackling something that may help your business grow, I encourage you to consider whether fear or self-doubt is really what is standing in your way. If so, follow the advice in this quote from Eleanor Roosevelt: "We gain strength, and courage, and confidence by each experience in which we really stop to look fear in the face . . . we must do that which we think we cannot."

## #7: Envy

While it is certainly wise to be thoroughly knowledgeable about the businesses you compete with day in and day out, it is also possible to waste valuable time comparing the status of your business with others. It is harmful to constantly fret over the success of your competitors or your friends rather than focusing on the more productive activities of building your business's core strengths and its client base.

The journey from being envious to being resentful of another person's business success can be a short but damaging trip. Envy is a negative emotion that can even produce uncertainty and instability in the way you run your business. Frequently adjusting how you operate to emulate what you've heard or read about someone else who seems to be soaring to the top will leave your customers confused and wondering just exactly who you are and what your business is about.

We should all have our business heroes, people we admire and emulate to the extent we can. But when the emotion we feel toward another business-person is more akin to the green-eyed monster of jealousy than it is to veneration, we set ourselves up for feelings of inadequacy and low self-esteem. If instead of inspiring you with new insights on how to take your business further your envy of another's success leaves you feeling like you'll never measure up, this can be very harmful indeed.

### Don't Judge Based on the Facade

The public image of solopreneurs and small business owners is often a carefully constructed facade that tells you very little, if anything, about what is actually going on inside that person's business. I should know because, as a public relations professional, I have helped build those facades!

Many, many people are skilled at projecting an image of success when, in fact, their business is struggling. Unless you've had a look at their bank account, you don't know whether that competitor you envy because they drive a new car, dress in designer clothes, and live in a house twice the size of yours is actually pulling in enough dough to pay for all that luxury or is in debt up to their eyebrows. Even in the big leagues of the corporate world, we can all recall companies that were considered high flyers that crashed and burned with little warning to those of us on the outside.

When things are going slower in your own business than you like them to, when it's harder to find clients and your cash flow is barely keeping you afloat, it is all too easy to look around and find someone else who seems to have it all going right for them. But what does that accomplish, besides making you feel inadequate?

People who are new to the world of self-employment can be particularly prone to envy. Many newbies start with no realistic notion of how long it will take for them to get their business off the ground and moving toward success. They look around and see friends, former work colleagues, or competitors who appear to be forging ahead at great speed, never realizing just how much time and effort those people have put into getting where they are now. In their start-up period, these people may have met with just as much rejection as the newbie now faces, but the newbie doesn't know that.

This is where it becomes important to have a good mentor, someone who has been there/done that in your field and can give you the cold hard truth about what it will take to achieve the goals you've set for yourself. With such a dose of reality under your belt, you're less likely to waste time being envious of others because you'll better understand that in all likelihood the path they had to walk to achieve their success was just as tough as the one you're walking now.

Freeing your thoughts of the negativity that comes with envy is an important step toward enabling you to gain trust in your own abilities to succeed. We each have our own path to walk. By not wasting time on envy, you will move more quickly along your path without worrying about whether you are capable of matching the success of others.

## #8: Impatience

In an era in which we frequently read about college dropouts who start tech companies and become millionaires (at least on paper) within months, it is difficult—yet critically important—to remember that this is not the way most businesses grow. One of the worst mistakes you can make when you join the ranks of the self-employed is to become impatient with how your business is moving forward.

One cause of such impatience early on may be that you started with unrealistic expectations. If you didn't do adequate research before hanging out your shingle, you may not understand how long and how hard it can be to build the thriving, growing business of your dreams.

Impatience leads to all sorts of other bad behaviors that can easily take you off track. If things don't happen fast enough for you, for example, you may become guilty of frequent second-guessing and unnecessary changes in direction. You may bail out on strategies or tactics before giving something, such as a new marketing platform, a realistic amount of time to work.

Impatience can cause you to take actions that will damage relationships with vendors and even clients. I've known more than one solopreneur who botched a prospective client relationship because they were simply too darn impatient when it came to making the sale. Prospects don't necessarily like to be bugged every day about when they're going to sign a contract. They'll do it according to their own schedule, which may not match up with your timetable—or with your strong financial need to get that deposit into your bank account.

Another side of this is that no vendor wants to work with a client who is constantly breathing down their neck. I personally have stopped working with clients who constantly exhibited this type of behavior toward me, their PR vendor. So if you're impatient with your own vendors, you may get kicked to the curb too.

If you hire subcontractors, impatience can cause problems with these relationships also. Yes, it's good to have a sense of urgency about getting work done in a timely fashion, but when impatience is the attitude you consistently bring to these work relationships, it can be very wearing on those around you. As I've mentioned, being able to choose your clients is one of the biggest benefits of being self-employed. Are subcontractors really going to choose you if you frequently exhibit signs of impatience?

## Good Mentors May Help

If you tend to be an impatient person in other aspects of your life, you may become even more so when it comes to your business because you have so much riding on the outcome. This is where having mentors can be a big help. People who have run their own businesses and/or have advised other solopreneurs know the wisdom of the "Rome wasn't built in a day" adage. They can help you head off the potential damage you might do if you're prone to frequent displays of impatience.

It would be wonderful if your business met with the type of instant success that produces headlines and would immediately put your financial concerns behind you. But for the majority of self-employed people, success is a high mountain to climb. Being impatient is unlikely to get you to the top sooner and may, in fact, impede your journey.

# CHAPTER THIRTY-TWO

# So What's Stopping You?

If you've stuck with me this far, it probably means that all this talk of challenges and coping strategies has not put you off the idea of being self-employed. Good for you! My goal is to make you better prepared, not to dissuade you from the idea of being your own boss. Now that you have a fuller appreciation for what self-employment is actually like on a day-to-day basis, I hope you will proceed with the work needed to prepare yourself to take this big step.

If you're still having doubts about whether you could make it on your own, please take time to identify specifically what aspects of self-employment seem most daunting to you. Reread the chapters that particularly hit home with you the first time you read them. Once you've identified what is scaring you enough to prompt you to consider putting away your dream of being your own boss, consider whether these may be issues that you can plan ahead for to reduce the potential for things to go wrong.

An example would be amassing a very healthy rainy-day fund in advance of starting your business if the thought of having periodic cash flow dips is what sets your nerves on edge. Or do you hate being alone for long stretches of time, as you would be in a home office? If so, one solution would be to find space in a coworking facility with office space that is affordable enough for a start-up business and offers the benefit of being part of a community of working professionals with whom you can network. Of course, renting space may mean you have to put together a bigger nest egg before you launch your business, but it might be worth it if it means you can avoid the downsides of working alone at home.

It is completely normal to have trepidations about making such a big change in your life; becoming self-employed is definitely going to shake things up. I would worry if you had absolutely no fears at this point because that may mean you're not being 100 percent realistic about the challenges that lie ahead. Having a high level of confidence is great unless it means you haven't carefully considered and planned for all the contingencies you'll face when you're your own boss.

Best wishes as you embark on your self-employment journey. May you have loads of luck and run into as few perils as possible. Do keep in touch through SucceedinginSmallBusiness.com and please share your stories of how you faced down the challenges of self-employment with me there. Bon voyage!

# Acknowledgments

Once I started coauthoring and ghostwriting books, dozens of people asked me when I was going to write a book of my own. Although I resisted the idea for nearly two decades, hearing that question over and over planted the seed that eventually grew into this book. So thanks to everyone who asked me that question over the years.

Thanks, of course, to my friends and colleagues who contributed directly to the book. Please read their bios, visit their websites, and follow them on social media. They are all great at what they do.

Thanks also to the many unnamed people, including friends and clients, who taught me how to succeed at self-employment. From some I learned by watching their good example. In other cases, I witnessed people struggle and saw what didn't work, which is often just as good a way to learn as by having a good example to follow.

Thanks to Steve Harris of CSG Literary Partners for responding quickly and enthusiastically when he received a book proposal and manuscript from someone he'd never heard of. His hard work found the right home for my book at Rowman & Littlefield, and I will be forever grateful. Thanks as well to Suzanne Staszak-Silva and everyone else at Rowman & Littlefield who worked so hard to make this book a reality.

Finally, no mention of my work as a writer would be complete without a big nod to my mother, Kathleen Campbell Yocum, a high school English and literature teacher who set me on the path to being a writer from my earliest days. Just as my father led me toward self-employment by his daily example, Mother inspired me to pursue a career in which writing has been a major component of my self-fulfillment. That neither of them lived long enough to see a book with my name on the cover is one of my life's greatest regrets.

# Index

# About the Author and Contributors

**Jeanne Yocum** has been self-employed as a ghostwriter and public relations consultant since 1989. In 2010, she launched a blog called SucceedingIn SmallBusiness.com, where she and her cobloggers offer advice on self-employment and small business ownership.

Jeanne's published works include two coauthored books, *New Product Launch: 10 Proven Strategies*, written with Joan Schneider, and *Ban the Humorous Bazooka and Other Roadblocks and Speed Bumps along the Innovation Highway*, written with Mark Sebell. She has also ghostwritten five business books on topics such as open innovation, strategic partnerships, and entrepreneurship, and has edited several other books.

Jeanne holds a bachelor's degree in Journalism from Pennsylvania State University and a master's degree in Journalism from Boston University. Born in Pennsylvania, she spent most of her career in Massachusetts before moving to Durham, North Carolina, in 2013.

**Mark G. Auerbach** is principal of Mark G. Auerbach Public Relations, which has provided strategic planning and hands-on campaign management for a variety of marketing, advertising, public relations, special events, and development projects since 1987.

Mark's clients have included broadcast media programs and outlets, performing arts organizations, travel organizations and programs, authors, and educational institutions. Mark balances his business by working as an arts reporter for several print, web, and radio outlets. A native of Longmeadow,

Massachusetts, Mark studied at Northfield Mount Hermon School, American University, and the Yale School of Drama.

**Holly Gonzalez** is an independent copywriter and marketing strategist with more than twenty years of experience, specializing in marketing communications. A native South Floridian, she grew up in Coral Gables. Now based in Austin, Texas, her clients include advertising agencies, design firms, and corporate clients throughout Texas, Florida, and New England. Prior to launching her freelance copywriting business, Holly served as director of special events and public relations for advertising and public relations agencies in Miami and Boston. She earned her bachelor's degree in Psychology from Smith College. For more information visit www.hollygonzalez.com.

**Howie Green** is an illustrator and designer located in Boston, Massachusetts. He has received more than forty-five awards for his work for Fortune 500 and regional clients, including Coca-Cola, LL Bean, CBS TV, *New Age Journal*, and many others. He has written two books, including the category best-seller *Jazz Fish Zen: Adventures in Mamboland*. As an internationally recognized painter, his work has appeared in more than forty-five group and solo gallery shows, and he has created more than fifty public murals and art projects for clients, including the Cow Parade Boston, Sun Life Financial, the Mayor's Office of Boston, and the Boston Red Sox Foundation. See more of Howie's work at www.hgd.com.

**Stefan Lindegaard** is a Copenhagen-based author, speaker, strategic adviser, and entrepreneur. His focus on corporate transformation, digitalization, and innovation management based on leadership, the work force, and organizational structures has propelled him into being a trusted source of inspiration to many large corporations, government organizations, and smaller companies around the world.

In his role as a strategic adviser and coach, Stefan provides external perspectives and practical advice for executives and their corporate transformation, digitalization, and innovation teams. He is a widely respected writer and has written several books, including *The Open Innovation Revolution* published globally. You can follow his work on LinkedIn Pulse. Most recently, Stefan is the cofounder and Chief Thought Leader of Transform XO—a thought-leadership-driven think tank and accelerator with a special focus on digital capabilities for corporate innovation. You can read more on Transform XO.

**Pat Mullaly** has been an entrepreneur since establishing her graphic design firm, Circle Graphics, in 1986. Located just south of Boston, she has focused on developing collateral materials, corporate identity, and websites for small businesses and nonprofits. Working with a network of writers, photographers, programmers, and website wizards, Pat has successfully managed to meet or exceed the demands of all her clients. An avid golfer, she created GolfGurls .com in 2009 to share this passion. A popular resource for golfers around the globe, this is a website for today's woman golfer, featuring tips, training, and product reviews. Visit GolfGurls.com or learn about Pat's graphic design work at CircleGraphics.com.

**Barbara Rodriguez** is an entrepreneur, educator, and businesswoman who has grown two successful businesses, one that addresses a critical aspect of health care—the growing need for medical interpreters to ensure that patients with limited English skills receive quality care. Starting with what she had—bilingual abilities and business skills training—Barbara decided to address the growing need for quality translation and interpreting services. With no start-up money and while still in graduate school, she worked out of her home, initially servicing a small roster of area clients.

The Springfield Small Business Incubator (SBI), which provides support and resources to early-stage businesses, accepted Barbara as a tenant in 2006. While at SBI, TransFluenci took off, doubling in revenues and number of contracts. Today, it is recognized as a leading interpreter and translation services company and is one of the largest and most successful firms in the region, handling translations and interpretations for corporations, legal firms, hospitals, and human services agencies, among many other clients. Her spinoff company, TransFluenciEDU, offers a medical interpreting certificate course in partnership with eight Massachusetts community colleges, and she has recently launched an online version of the medical interpreting course. Visit www.transfluenci.com or www.transfluenciedu.com for more information.

**Carol Savage** is a public relations and marketing communications freelance professional located in Ipswich, Massachusetts. An award-winning writer and publicist, Carol has thirty-plus years of experience planning, writing, and implementing corporate communications and public relations programs. She has worked with clients in health care, hospitality, construction, manufacturing, and business-to-business, as well as with major nonprofit organizations. Carol has won writing awards for marketing collateral from national associations and the regional chapter of the Society for Marketing Professionals.

Carol earned a master's degree in Corporate Public Relations from Boston University's College of Communications and an undergraduate degree in English and History from Emmanuel College. She is a member of the Public Relations Society of America. For more information, visit www.carolsavage-communications.com.